REV. STACEY SARTIN

HAPPY
Sunday!

Because Every Day is "Son"Day

House Capacity Publishing
Support@housecapacity.com
www.housecapacity.com

Printed in the United States of America

ISBN-13: 978-1-0879-1065-9

This daily devotional is dedicated to everyone who needs Jesus every day of their lives.

To the faithful in Christ who know and understand that every day is Son Day.

Happy Sunday!

January 1

An octopus will detach an arm for a predator to escape its grasp and grow back a new one later.

It's better to let go of things that are replaceable than to lose everything trying to keep them.

Be armed with Godly wisdom.

January 2

a hippopotamus is born underwater and spends the rest of its life dipping in and out of the water, but they cannot live underwater because that is not their true nature to do so.

Likewise, as Believers we are born in sin and, being imperfect, commit sins throughout our lives, but we do not live in sin because it is not our true nature to do so.

That's why Jesus died for us, because we are unable to stay out of the water; but don't take advantage of His sacrifice—try to stay as dry as you can.

Romans 6:1, 2 New Living Translation: "What shall we say then? Shall we keep on sinning so that God can show us more and more of his wonderful grace? Of course not!

HAPPY *Sunday!*

January 3

SCAN ME

*R*ainbows represent the promises of God. In order to see a rainbow, three things must occur: the Sun must be behind you, it must be raining, and you must be looking up.

When the Sun strikes the rain, it penetrates the rain drops and breaks down light as it reflects back at us. When the light breaks down, it reveals all of the colors we cannot see with the naked eye— hence the rainbow.

When it's raining problems in our lives, if the Son is behind us, and we are looking up, the Light of God will shine through those problems and reveal the promises of God that we couldn't see before.

So if you ask Jesus to have your back, and look up - through the problems you're facing - His Light will shine through your problems, and you'll see the promises of God that you couldn't see before.

I love you in the name of Jesus Christ. Look up, even it's raining in your life and see the rainbow of God!

January 4

Kangaroos struggle and stumble when they walk backwards. This is their weakness.

God has made us the same way. We were made to leap up and forward—always—in faith towards Him. This gives us strength.

We struggle and stumble when we back away from Him. This makes us weak.

Take a leap of faith today and be strong in the Lord going forward.

January 5

*T*he line of sight to the cloud of rain that creates your rainbow is different from that of the person next to you. Everybody sees his or her own personal rainbow.

Rainbows represent the promises of God.

The line of sight to the promises of God in your life is different from that of the person next to you. So don't doubt God's promises to you because someone else can't see them; they're supposed to see things differently.

What God has for you is for you.

January 6

a human voice can shatter glass by singing and holding a note that has the same frequency of the glass.

The power is derived by maintaining the note and taking on the same vibration as the glass.

A human spirit can shatter a stronghold by praying according to God's Word and moving according to His will.

The power is in maintaining your faith and taking on the same vibes as our Creator.

Shatter your strongholds today.

January 7

*T*he Honey Badger is a ferocious snake killer. It owes its fearlessness to an inherited blood mutation that overcomes snake venom.

It has few natural predators because of its defensive tenacity and thick skin, which is so loose that it allows the honey badger to twist and turn freely within it.

It is considered one of the least endangered animals in the world because of its unique fighting capabilities and its ability to adapt to different environments.

Like honey badgers, Believers are more than conquerors when it comes to serpents. We owe our victories to Jesus whose blood has made us clean from the sin that had poisoned us.

As Believers, we're given power to love in

all situations, and we have thick skin which allows us to freely move in prayer and faith—even under vicious attack.

We're able to turn from sin and destruction, and look to God for strength and help in time of trouble.

Even when bitten, we have confession and repentance as a reviving anti-venom.

So get a little spiritual ferocity about yourself. Yes, the devil may be attacking, but you're a honey badger in Jesus and invincible in Christ!

January 8

*V*ents allow heat to come out the wall a room. When a room is cold, the vent is opened; if it's warm, the vent is closed and the heat stays in the wall.

Our mouths are like vents. When people are warm to us, we usually keep our vent closed because there is no need to let out heat. When people do cold things, it leads us to open the vent and let out a little heat.

That's how things get heated.

Today, consider the temperature of each conversation carefully, and don't let out heat unless it's absolutely necessary.

That's how you stop things from getting heated.

January 9

*W*hen Helium is cooled to almost absolute zero, the lowest temperature possible, it becomes a liquid, flows upward against gravity, and will start running up and over the lip of a glass container!

As Believers, when things get heated in our lives, we stay cool. The peace of God lifts us, and sees us through whatever has us bound until we're able to get up and over it.

So stay cool and praise God (in my helium voice).

January 10

*W*hen the angel Gabriel told Mary she was favored by God and that the son of God would come into the world through her, she agreed with God's will for her and said to the angel, "May it be unto me as you have said."

The world and Mary were blessed forever by her humble free-will decision.

Today, Jesus is telling us the Spirit of God will be in us as a blessing to ourselves and the world around us if we freely accept Him as Savior.

May we all have the wisdom and urging of the Spirit to be as wise as Mary.

January 11

*T*here is enough DNA in an average person's body to stretch from the sun to Pluto and back—17 times.

See how wonderfully we are made?

God has put enough in us to be able reach out to Him no matter how far we tend to stray, nor how many times we do it, as long as our lives revolve around the Son.

We all sin (fall away at times); less and less, but still over and over again, as God sanctifies us to Himself. The sacrifice of Jesus atones for it all, when we confess and repent, and the love of God draws us back in forgiveness, mercy, and grace, with Jesus Christ as the center of our lives.

HAPPY *Sunday!*

January 12

Stomach acid is strong enough to dissolve razor blades.

Spiritually, that speaks to how God has made us in such a way that even if things are hard to swallow and cut to the gut, we can survive and eventually get past them.

Whatever it is you're having a problem digesting, trust God to solve it, and trust what He put inside you to dissolve it.

January 13

*W*hen you drink, you swallow because you know whatever you are drinking will go down. That is how drinking and swallowing works.

When you pray, you believe because you know whatever you pray will go down. That is how praying and believing works.

Mark 11:24 New International Version- Therefore I tell you, whatever you ask for in prayer, believe that you have received it, and it will be yours.

Don't drink if you're not going to swallow, and don't pray if you're not going to believe. It doesn't work that way.

January 14

a s a child, my parents gave me a television without a remote control. If I didn't like what I was watching, I had to get up and change the channel myself.

Today, as a child of God, I've been given new life in Christ but God isn't going to remotely start changing things just because I don't like what my world looks like.

If I don't like what I see in my life, He has given me the strength, power, and wisdom to get up and change it myself.

If you don't like what you see in your life, in Jesus' name get up and change the channels, because the chances of them changing on their own are definitely highly remote.

January 15

*E*ver notice that no matter how deep you're sleeping, you physically wake up when sunlight hits you?

The same thing happens when Son light hits you. You wake up spiritually, no matter how deep asleep you were.

John 8:12 - When Jesus spoke again to the people, he said, "I am the light of the world...."

January 16

*T*he Ark of the Covenant signified the presence of God among the ancient Hebrews. The two poles used to lift it were Holy and remained connect to the ark.

Today, the two poles are represented by our faith and works. They lift the presence of God wherever we go. Both are to remain in our ark, Jesus Christ, the expressed presence of God in our lives.

Exodus 25:15 - "The poles shall remain in the rings of the ark; they shall not be removed from it..."

Keep your poles in the ark.

January 17

*W*hen you give up, God gives down. So if you have given up and things have gone down, don't blame God for what's going down, because you're responsible for giving up.

Stop giving up, and the things hindering your blessings will stop going down.

That's what's up, whatever is going down.

January 18

*P*eople change in two ways: they stop or start doing something, or you stop or start seeing them doing something.

Meaning people can change but you can't change people because the only thing that changes is what you see in people – as what you see changes.

So if people have changed, or you're looking for change in them, I hope this changes how you see the change in them, because that is how things will change.

January 19

*T*hings may be going well in one area of your life and not so well in another. That's because, like Earth, different areas in our world require different seasons relative to their position to the Son.

Just trust God and continue to let everything revolve around Him. Seasons change.

January 20

*J*esus stayed on the cross because He was nailed there. That is how He was able to maintain the sacrifice He was making for us. Otherwise, even the slightest reaction to the pain and suffering He underwent (for us) would have caused Him to fall off.

He was showing us that we, too, need something to maintain the sacrifices we make for those we love. We need something to hold us to these sacrifices.

Nails held Him to His cross; His Words hold us to ours. So hammer the Word of God as deep into your heart and mind as He allowed the Romans to drive nails into His hands and feet.

This is how you bear the cross, secured by the Spirit through the world. This way you won't fall off from the sacrifices you are making (in His name) for those you love.

January 21

B aby Steps

Don't beat yourself up about past sins. Walking with God begins with baby steps. Babies fall a lot.

Keep trying, doing better, getting back up, and holding onto things that help you balance and stand.

Remember, you were carried, then crawled, then walked, then ran. One day soon you'll fly and soar.

Trust the process of holiness. It's called sanctification.

HAPPY *Sunday!*

January 22

*T*ears blur and distort your vision in such a way that makes it hard to see things, even if you focus on them. However, focusing on something with your vision also focuses your mind, which takes your mind off of what made you cry. Removing your focus from what made you cry stops the crying and dries the tears. When the tears dry, things begin to return to focus and clear up.

Hopefully it's clear that I'm telling you to focus on Jesus if you are crying. Even if it's not clear how He will fix it, if you focus on Him, your mind will stay on Him and be off whatever made you cry. When the tears dry, you will see that having your mind stayed on Jesus has given you perfect peace.

January 23

$\mathcal{G}$rasshoppers are weak and no threat by themselves, but in swarms they are a devastating and formidable force. This is because each is its own leader, led from within to form a whole.

Outside of the will of God and left to our own purposes, we are weak. When we move in the body of Jesus Christ, all power is wielded through us. This is because the Spirit of God within us, allows us to work out our own salvation as we edify the body of Christ as a whole.

The grasshoppers don't have a king that you can see with your eyes, because he rules from inside them. You see their king in the effects of their actions. It is the same with us and our King, Jesus.

January 24

U nlike most birds, eagles are not afraid of storms. Instead of hiding from them, they use the strong air currents to fly higher and rise above it; they soar to new heights through storms.

Have eagle faith today. Don't hide from the storm nor be afraid of it. Face it and rise above it; soar to new heights.

Isaiah 40:31 – "...mount up with wings as eagles..."

January 25

$\mathcal{S}$ omeday can be any day you make it. If you have been waiting on someday to do something, make someday today; it's as good a day any day, especially if you're depending on Jesus, because:

"Jesus Christ the same yesterday, and today, and forever."

(Paul's pastoral letter to the Hebrews, chapter thirteen, verse eight)

So if you do what you were waiting to do someday today, it will be some day, quite a glorious day—in Jesus.

January 26

W hen a carpenter ant is under attack and fears it is about to lose, it explodes.

That is why it is best not to argue with people, because most are like carpenter ants; once they fear they are losing the argument, they start to blow up and explode.

Philippians 2:14 New International Version – "Do everything without grumbling or arguing."

Try not to blow up today. Hold your peace in disagreements, even the ones you feel you're losing.

January 27

*T*he angler fish spits beads of water at insects flying overhead in order to knock them down and eat them.

There are people in our lives spitting out all types of things at us to knock us down and devour us, also.

Stay prayed up and beware of anyone acting fishy.

January 28

$\mathcal{T}$he electric eel uses two different voltages: 10 volts for electro-location (to find out what's in its environment as it moves through it) and 500 volts to keep predators away.

In the same vein, God provides believers with two powers, too: the power to discern what is going on around us and power to keep our enemies at bay.

Unlike the electric eel, that shouldn't be shocking because God is good and has all power.

January 29

... *L*ord save me!

(Peter's cry to Jesus as he began to sink as He walked toward Jesus on water)

The Bible says Peter began to sink when he "saw the wind," and cried out to Jesus for help; however, we cannot see wind. We see and hear the effects of wind; we feel it.

Peter sank because he feared the effects of the wind.

We too often sink away from God and the miraculous walk He has commanded for us simply because we fear some of the effects see surrounding that walk.

Have faith, God won't let you sink. Jesus call us to walk any path in which He won't keep and protect us. The only things that can sink us are our fears, worries, and doubts.

Today, ignore the sound effects and walk on and over whatever leads you to Jesus. He waiting, and if you start to slip He is only a cry away.

January 30

*I*n the Bible, there was a prophet that was cutting down a tree to build a home when his axe handle flew off, fell into a river, and sank. Worried because the axe was borrowed and he would not be able to finish building, He went to the man of God for help.

The man of God took a new piece of wood and threw it into the river. Immediately, the axe head began to rise up and the prophet was able to use it again because of the new handle the man of God had provided.

God can do the same thing in your life. If you are trying to build something in your life and suddenly lose your handle on things, turn to the manifestation of God in our lives - Jesus Christ.

He will replace what you were using to keep a handle on things with something that doesn't fall off. He will get you building again—Kingdom building and whatever else needs building up in your life.

January 31

*W*hen I hold a balloon on a string, even though the balloon itself is not in my hand, I still feel the same ownership as if it was. That is because I am connected to the balloon in such a way that I can pull it into my hand at anytime. This leaves me free to hold and enjoy other things, knowing that with just a simple tug, I can retrieve my balloon at any time.

In our spiritual lives, the joy of our salvation works the same way. Our joy is in God the Father through His Risen Son, Christ Jesus, who connects us to the Father as we hold on through the Holy Spirit. This leaves us free to go through whatever we face knowing that God, through Christ Jesus, is only a tug away.

February 1

A nyone who has played a game of pool knows that when a ball bounces from a surface, it bounces away from the surface at an angle equal to the one in which it approached the surface.

The ball is obeying The Law of Reflection: the angle of reflection equals the angle of incidence.

Anyone who knows of Jesus Christ knows He loved us and laid down His life for us. That is how He came at us.

The law of Jesus Christ is that we love one another.

Accordingly, we who have received Christ should be coming off to others the same way He came off to us - loving others and laying down our lives to help them with theirs.

We should be obeying The Spiritual Law of Reflection—The Law of Love in Christ Jesus.

Take a shot at that today.

February 2

l ove conquers hate.

If you love to give, it will conquer the hate on your finances

If you love to make peace, it will conquer the confusion and strife in your life.

If you love encouraging and edifying others, it will conquer the gossip and lies about you.

If you love others, it will conquer the hate they have for you.

God is love. If you love and trust Him, it will conquer the fears, worries, and doubts you have about love conquering hate.

Romans 12:21— "Be not overcome of evil, but overcome evil with good."

I love you in the name of our Lord and Savior Jesus Christ whose love has conquered all things.

February 3

*L*eaves fall when the nutrients they receive from the branch is cut off. They change colors and fall from the elevated position they hold toward the Sun to the dirt and Earth below.

When we let go of the teachings of Jesus Christ and ignore the voice of His Spirit, we fall into the dirty things that used to be beneath us; a lowered character and morals, and worldly nature (true colors) start to reveal themselves. We no longer reach for the things of God, and wind up being trampled in the very things (mounds of dirt) we once grew out of.

Leaves don't have a choice; Fall is their season to fall, so fall what they do.

God has given us free will. Use it to hold onto Jesus Christ, the Branch of Jesse, and the True Vine. He is the Son of God and this is your season, so hold on by the Spirit and don't fall.

February 4

S ome people are like dark clouds without rain; they darken the days of others yet never do anything to help clean others up and never drop any knowledge that would quench the thirst others have for wisdom. All they live for is the shade they cast upon the lives of others.

Make sure that isn't you, all dark and cloudy over others with nothing to give but shade.

Jude 1:12 "...clouds they are without water, carried about with winds..."

February 5

*L*ions hunt together and bring their food home. When one lion has food, the whole family eats.

A family of lions is called a pride, which puts some families of humans to shame and that is nothing to be proud of, yet they have so much pride.

That is a shame. We should all be like lions and regain our pride.

Love one another. Help one another. Share what you have.

February 6

A trick on predators in the animal kingdom is to stay so close together in herds, that the enemy can't tell who or what to attack.

In our world, if we stay just as close, the same can be done for us. If one is hungry but is fed by another, how can the devil starve us? If one is falling and another catches, how can the devil trip us up? If one is in the dark, but another shines light, how can the devil blind us?

If we herd together as sheep before our Good Shepherd Christ Jesus, nothing will separate us from the love of God in Him.

So let's pull closer—just like a herd—so close that one can't fall for the other.

HAPPY *Sunday!*

February 7

*W*hen you pour water into dirt it triggers the growth of whatever seeds are planted in that dirt.

When you pour the word of God into a life buried in dirt, it triggers the growth of whatever seeds God planted in that life.

No matter how dirty your life or past, pour the Word into it and watch good things begin to grow out of it.

February 8

I n the Bible Jacob and Laban made a deal for cattle but Laban took all the striped and spotted cattle (the stronger ones) and left Jacob with all of the plain old regular cattle. God told Jacob to gather sticks and paint stripes and spots on the regular cattle and trust Him. When the plain cattle mated with the ones Jacob had painted, they produced striped and spotted offspring, and Jacob was able to replace all that Laban had taken. Even though genetics doesn't work that way, for Jacob it did.

God does the same for us when we brush over material loss, and gather up enough faith to dot our hearts in hope in and paint our minds in the trust that God will supply every need. When that type of faith mixes with whatever we have, it builds and replaces all that is missing. Even though it's not supposed to work that way, for those who love God it does.

February 9

*F*light isn't the only honor of being a bird. Some don't fly. For birds that don't fly, their honor is found in their strut; the walk that moves them forward.

Soaring to great heights of worldly achievement is not the only honor of a man. Not all men soar to great worldly achievements. For men that don't strive for such, their dignity and honor are found in the way they walk; their love for God and the reflection of that love as they move forward through life.

God will honor all you do in Him - anytime, anywhere, any level.

February 10

*I*n the Bible, Rahab went from harlot to ancestral mother in the bloodline of Jesus.

No matter what you're doing or have done, God can clean you up and bring incredible blessings out of you. He can take the dirty names you've been called and turn them into words of praise.

These glorious things happened to Rahab because she accepted what God sent to her house - spies in the name of the Lord. Even more glorious things can come your way. All you have to do is accept what God has sent to your house—salvation in the name of Jesus Christ.

February 11

*L*ifting a barbell as an exercise builds strength you can use to lift other things like the couch-end at home when you're vacuuming, or the groceries you bring in the house.

Trusting God in the little things exercises your faith and makes it strong enough to handle the bigger issues, concerns, and obstacles in life.

If you're not exercising your faith you will become weak, even in everyday things.

February 12

E ver wonder why you can feel someone looking at you? No, it's not ESP. It's called gaze perception. It's a natural ability to detect clues such as the direction of someone's head and body. The contrast between the pupil and sclera (white part of the eye) are designed in a way to tell if someone is looking at you or past you.

Now consider this: we are made in God's image. If we can tell if someone is looking at us, or not, surely we can't fool God.

If you aren't looking to God for salvation, don't fake it—He can tell.

February 13

*I*f you get change for a dollar, whatever the makeup of the change, it will still spend the same.

In the same vein, sometimes we look for change in others, whatever it may be, and when we get it, it still feels the same.

That doesn't mean shouldn't look for change; it just means don't always expect more than what you already had.

February 14

*T*he Lord is my keeper:

He keeps protecting me, He keeps filling me, He keeps blessing me, He keeps healing me, He keeps changing me, He keeps delivering me, He keeps leading me, He keeps guiding me, He keeps covering me, He keeps comforting me, He keeps lifting me, He keeps holding me, He keeps strengthening me, He keeps anointing me, He keeps cleansing me, He keeps...

Get the picture?

I could keep going, but I don't want to keep you. I just want you to know that He keeps keeping me.

Find Him if you haven't, and don't lose Him if you have—for the Lord is a keeper, and He will keep keeping you.

Psalm 121:5 – "The Lord is thy keeper..."

February 15

*Z*ebras only go to sleep when they are close to other zebras; this way, they can be warned when danger is near or predators are approaching.

As Christians, things rest better with us when we're in fellowship with each other because that's how we look out for each other.

If you're a Believer, have a restful and blessed day; I'm praying and looking out for you, please do the same for me!

February 16

*B*ehind chimpanzees, dolphins, and elephants, pigs are the smartest animals in the world.

So if you enjoy being fat in faith, greedy for the Word, wallowing in love, and pigging out on praise—you're pretty smart.

Go ahead— keep pigging out in Christ!

February 17

*I*n a novel way of drying itself, the kestrel, a tiny bird of prey, spins it head to shake off rain.

We, too, should learn to put a faithful spin on things when it rains in our lives and our minds get soaked with worry.

Trust God. Always hope and look for the best. Don't let this world dampen your spirit.

February 18

*I*ce melts at the same temperature water freezes.

Likewise, new life begins at the same point (belief in Jesus Christ) your old life ends.

So if you're at the point where you're about to melt down, you're in the best place to begin believing and chilling out in Jesus Christ.

February 19

*I*n the darkest physical hour, the moon (that big dead rock in the sky) rises and reflects the Sun's light, allowing us to see and make our way in the night.

In the darkest spiritual hour, the biggest and hardest things looming over our heads will also reflect light from the Son, allowing us to see through the dark times and make our way through night seasons.

God is faithful to those who love and trust Him; He makes a way in dark times. Love Him. Trust Him. He will make a way, even in your darkest hour.

February 20

*J*esus' first public miracle occurred when He turned water to wine at a wedding. He ordered an empty vessel be filled with water, then turned the water into wine that was better than that which had run out.

Today, Jesus performs the same miracle when He becomes your Lord and Savior. He takes your empty life and fills it with things that lift your spirit and bring you joy - more than there was before it ran out.

February 21

*M*eerkats eat toxic and poisonous prey like millipedes and scorpions, so they teach their pups to remove stingers and toxins at an early age.

Some of our youth today don't understand you can date without having sex. They don't know you can party without drugs and alcohol. They're not aware you can socialize without verbally attacking and fighting each other.

Perhaps we should consider the meerkat, and teach our young to remove toxins and stingers at an early age.

February 22

U UU.

UUUUUUUUUUUUUUUUUUUUUUUU
UUUUUUUUUUUUUUUUUUUUUUUU
UUUUUUUUUUUUUUUUU

UUU.

Just thought U might like to see how silly and pointless it looks when everything is all about U.

If U see U in this somewhere, start thinking about others.

Philippians 2:4 – "Look not every man on his own things, but every man also on the things of others."

February 23

*W*aking you up this morning was on God's LOVE To-Do List, not HAD To-Do List.

So be thankful for another day and praise His Holy Name.

That is not something you have to do, but it something you should love to do.

February 24

The best way to slow down a runaway horse is to turn it in a wide circle and keep circling in smaller circles until the horse stops.

Once he is calm, you can restart the trail again.

The best way to slow down a runaway social life is to turn from a wide circle of friends and keep trimming that circle until only true and loyal friends remain in the circle.

Once you have peace, you can start a new life from there.

February 25

*T*hink of the Bible as a gym where we can work off excess weight and burdens. We all have a membership, but some of us never go.

That's why our hearts are still heavy, and our lives overburdened. That's why we run short of breath and words to say, when we need God the most. That's why we end up sweating everything, even the slightest and simplest tasks (love, forgiveness...).

So get back in the Bible. You'll develop a stronger heart for God, and your life will be in better shape.

February 26

*G*od is an awesome artist. Whenever I confess and repent of my sins, He forgives me and draws a blank.

Hebrews 8:12 – "For I will be merciful to their unrighteousness, and their sins and their iniquities will I remember no more."

February 27

*W*hen a bird bends its knees and lands on a branch, its feet curl and lock into place. As long as the bird's knees are bent, the feet are locked onto the branch— leaving the bird in an elevated position and safe from any danger below. As Believers, Jesus is the Branch on which we rest. When we bend our knees in prayer and rest in obedience, our spirits lock into His. As we continue in Him through perpetual prayer while humbling ourselves in His Word, our souls are locked into heavenly places— safe from all alarms.

February 28

*H*eat never of itself flows from a cold object to a hot object. This scientific fact is the Second Law of Thermodynamics.

If you're on fire for Jesus and someone is cold towards God, they may never warm up to you.

That is something we need to understand, acknowledge, and accept.

March 1

*T*he atomic nucleus of an atom occupies only a few quadrillionths of the volume of the atom. Outside of the atomic nucleus, there is most empty space.

Unbeknownst to those who haven't made God the nucleus of their lives, there is mostly empty space outside of Him, too. That is why life feels so empty without Him; God is what fills it up.

Make God the nucleus of your life.

March 2

Some planets like Jupiter and Saturn can be visited but you can't land and rest on them because they have no solid surface upon which to land. They are made up mostly of liquid and gas.

The reason some of us are so spaced out and unable to settle down is because we are trying to find rest in places where there is no solid foundation – no place to land. Now that's a gas.

So come out of that world and orbit Jesus. He is a Rock upon which to stand. He is land— a promised One.

March 3

*T*here are poisonous snakes in every state. Only the massasauga can be found in Michigan, the state in which I live.

That's good to know because when you don't know the snakes around you, you live in a state of ignorance.

Knowing the snakes around you puts you in a better state; a better state of mind, health, and being.

The Serpent has children everywhere. So get to know the snakes around you, and stop being bitten by what you think are friends. Get out of that ignorant state.

HAPPY *Sunday!*

March 4

*T*ime does not give refunds or refills, so spend it wisely and try not to waste it.

March 5

*n*o matter what sin you committed yesterday, if God woke you up this morning, you have a second chance.

Take it.

The sin you committed is one for which He died and the chance you have to be forgiven today is one for which He rose.

Confess, repent, and move forward in Christ.

March 6

*E*ver realize we complain with the same breath that keeps us alive? With the same mouth that feeds us?

Ever think about walking away from God using the legs He gave us to get around? Going someplace else like He isn't there, too?

How can we not look to the God who gave us eyes to see? How can we not listen to Him with the ears He put on our heads?

Let's think about those questions with the mind He gave us.

March 7

*J*ustifying ourselves before God with good works is like trying to sweep all the dirt out the forest.

Only the blood of Jesus can make us clean.

March 8

*W*hen floodwaters rise, insects are washed into the water and fish eat the insects.

When floodwaters recede, fish are left on the land and insects eat the fish.

The lesson in this?

When the waters of life start to rage and overtake boundaries that keep them back, don't be so quick to let them engulf you nor so eager to rise up in them.

Sinking or rising to either level will destroy or eventually devour you, because they both feed off each other.

March 9

*I*n life, like in baseball, you don't have to swing at everything thrown at the plate.

If someone or something changes up on you, throws you a curve, or tries to slip a fast one by you, don't lunge foolishly trying to connect with it; sit back and let God call it for what it really is.

He has an eye on every pitch, and it's a ball when you get your call.

March 10

*J*esus' disciples could not heal a young man through prayer so they asked Jesus why they failed.

Jesus told them that some things require more than prayer, they also require fasting.

It frustrated Jesus that they lacked faith and gave up without doing more; as if prayer was the only tool at their disposal.

The disciples should have known to do more; they should have kept using the tools Jesus had given them to glorify God until their faith allowed one or a combination of those tools to solve the problem. Instead, they came to Him asking why the tools did not work when they had only used prayer with weak faith.

Today, be sure you are not frustrating Jesus by giving up on something without using all the tools in Christ you have at your disposal. Pray, fast, love, forgive, be kind, be meek, control yourself, seek counsel...do all you can to solve a problem before you go to the Lord saying the power you have in His name doesn't work.

March 11

*M*ost young animals look like smaller versions of their parents. Kittens look like small cats. Puppies look like small dogs. Other young animals don't look like their parents at all.

Take insects for example. A butterfly, like many insects, has to go through a metamorphosis—a change that includes several growth stages.

That is why we shouldn't judge others, and say they aren't children of God based on how they look at a given moment in time. They may be children of God who have not gone through their metamorphosis (the regeneration/sanctification process).

March 12

*L*ot's wife was delivered from the sin and destruction behind her, but never reached where she was trying to go because she turned back and was turned into salt.

If you've been delivered from a life of sin that was leading to destruction, don't look back. It will prevent you from getting to where you're trying to go and that will make you salty.

March 13

a woman once poured expensive oil on Jesus as a sign of her love for Him. Those standing by began to complain that she was wasting the oil, saying that it could have been sold and the money spent on more important things.

Jesus rebuked them and she carried on doing what she was doing.

In our lives, others will see us pouring out our best to Jesus and think that we should sell out Christ and spend our time and efforts on things they believe are more important.

Jesus will rebuke them, too, so carry on doing just what you're doing as a sign of love for Him.

March 14

Running in water is difficult because the water fights against you as you do it. Trying it will exhaust you and make you stop running in water.

Trying to serve God as you live an unGodly life is difficult because the things you do fight against the things you think. Trying to live this way will exhaust you and make you stop serving God.

Walk in the Spirit.

Romans 8:8,9 – "...they that are in the flesh cannot please God. But ye are not in the flesh, but in the Spirit, if so be that the Spirit of God dwell in you..."

March 15

I broke the law and couldn't be fixed but Jesus fixed the law and now I can't be broken:

Romans 8:2 – "For the law of the Spirit of life in Christ Jesus hath made me free from the law of sin and death."

Amen

Because Every Day is "Son"day.

March 16

Sowing a seed is not the only way to grow a plant. Some plants, such as ferns and mosses, use spores instead of seeds to make new plants. A spore is a cell in a seedless plant that can grow into a new plant.

So if you want to help someone or something grow and you don't have money to "sow a seed," give a spore (part of your time or talent). That is the same as sowing a seed.

March 16

Sowing a seed is not the only way to grow a plant. Some plants, such as ferns and mosses, use spores instead of seeds to make new plants. A spore is a cell in a seedless plant that can grow into a new plant.

So if you want to help someone or something grow and you don't have money to "sow a seed," give a spore (part of your time or talent). That is the same as sowing a seed.

March 17

*G*od is in the night season all day long.

March 18

*W*hen you see a flying insect at a window trying to get out of the house, you don't always have to squash it.

Oftentimes you can just raise the window and it will fly away on its own.

Think about that when you have a beef with someone and you're considering how to squash it.

Matthew 5:9 – "Blessed are the peacemakers: for they shall be called the children of God."

Amen

March 19

*F*loor cable protectors are there to keep people from tripping and falling due to unseen cables and power cords laying in their paths.

Scripture works the same way.

If you keep it laid out before you, it will keep you from tripping and falling due to evil principalities and powers lying hidden in your path.

March 20

*S*criptures are like braces. If you put them in your mouth and leave them there for a while, they close gaps, straighten things out, and create a beautiful smile.

March 21

*I*f you're unable to rest at night because of your position, you switch positions until you find the rest you need.

If you can't find rest in life because of the position you've into which you've gotten yourself—switch positions until you find the rest you need.

Make the changes in life that will give you rest:

Matthew 11:28—"Come into me all ye that labor are heavy laden, and I will give you rest."

Amen

March 22

*W*ater going down a drain north of the equator will swirl in a counter-clockwise direction. Water going down a drain south of the equator will swirl in a clockwise direction.

Spiritual fact:

If God says things are not meant to be, they are not meant to be. No matter how far you go to change things, if they are meant to go down the drain, they will continue to go down the drain—one way or another.

Life Application:

Don't drain yourself trying not to drain yourself of the things God is trying to drain to keep you from being drained.

March 23

Sometimes you can focus so much on what you have lost that you lose sight of what you have.

Remember what you lost but look at what you have, then thank God for both.

March 24

You don't grow new muscles when you exercise; the muscles you have get bigger and stronger. So if you're weak and have little muscles, lift weights until they get bigger. That is a good workout plan.

In the same vein, you don't grow new faith; as you exercise the faith you already have, it grows bigger and stronger. So if you're in trouble and have little faith, that is a good work-it-out plan.

March 25

Some things need to be strained before you can begin serving them (e.g. boiled noodles and rice). This applies to spiritual things, also: love must be strained of hate, faith must be strained of worry, and hope must be strained of doubt.

Love God, have faith, and put your hopes in Jesus Christ. Strain everything not of God.

That is when serving Him begins.

March 26

*G*od gave the three Hebrew boys in the fiery furnace the power to ignore the heat as they walked and talked with Him through the fire.

You have that same power through Christ Jesus.

No matter how heated your situation, walk and talk with God as you go through the fire.

That is how the Hebrew boys survived their fire, and that is how you will survive yours.

March 27

*W*alking on water is miraculous, but sometimes it's not the water that God gives us the ability to walk on— it's things He puts into the water that we're able to stand and move on.

So step out in faith. You may not be able to walk on water, but God will put things into whatever you step into that will hold you up and move you forward.

That is just as miraculous.

March 28

*W*hen a man-made object sits in one place too long, things made by God begin to grow right through them.

When you believe and trust in God, and man-made problems and obstacles are placed in your life, the things of God begin to grow right through them, too—things like faith, peace, comfort, and deliverance.

So if there is a problem or obstacle in your life that looks like it's not going anywhere anytime soon, let the things of God grow through it.

Soon, the problem or obstacle will be covered in things God raised up in you, and you won't even know it's still there.

God can fix things in ways we can't imagine. That is what He does.

HAPPY Sunday!

March 29

*W*hen I eat an appetizer I eat it to eat again, because I'm expecting a bigger plate and better helping to follow.

Bon appetite!

As I live this life I live it to live again because I am expecting a bigger (eternal) and better life to follow.

Praise the Lord!

March 30

*G*od is always straight with us, but He turns things at His own angles.

So trust Him, even when things don't seem straight, or when they turn at angles that surprise us.

His thoughts are above our thoughts and His ways above our ways, but they are always good and turn out right for those that love and trust Him.

March 31

*F*ear, worry, and doubt are the utensils the devil uses to eat away at your spirit.

Take away his eating utensils and Satan will starve, because God won't let Him put His hands on you.

April 1

*S*top trying to understand why you dislike some people for absolutely no good reason at all. Our hearts are wicked and beyond our understanding:

Jeremiah 17:9 - The heart is deceitful above all things, and desperately wicked: who can know it?

Instead, try to understand that God can give us new hearts that understand His love, and give us power to show that love to others:

HAPPY Sunday!

*E*zekiel 11:19 – "And I will give them one heart, and I will put a new spirit within you; and I will take the stony heart out of their flesh, and will give them an heart of flesh..."

You're not going to "like" everybody and everyone isn't going to like you, but God loves us all and in Him we can walk in that love - together:

John 17:21 - That they all may be one; as thou, Father, art in me, and I in thee, that they also may be one in us...

Understand that.

Amen

April 2

*D*espite the popularity of the phrase "happiness is just around the corner," happiness cannot be found around the corner in this world because it's round and has no corners.

You'll be looking forever, as some have.

Happiness is found in Jesus Christ, who for our sakes cornered the love of God and became the cornerstone of our Faith. Happiness is around Him.

Find that corner and stand on it; in turn, you'll be happy forever.

HAPPY *Sunday!*

April 3

a prophet and His servant were surrounded by a large energy force and the servant was frightened because of the size of the army they were facing.

The prophet, knowing and trusting God, asked Him to open the spiritual eyes of his servant so that he could see that there were more forces of God standing ready to fight for them than all of the forces coming against them.

God answered the prophet and opened the servant's eyes, bringing comfort to him when he saw (with his own eyes) that the forces of God working to protect them were vastly greater than those opposing them.

I'm no prophet in the ancient biblical sense, I'm a just a voice crying out the things of God, but today, if you are standing in fear, worry, or doubt because of the many troubles and threats surrounding you, I am praying that God opens your eyes so you can see that He who stands for you is vastly greater than anything opposing you.

Because Every Day is "Son"day.

I love you in the name of Jesus.

2 Kings 6:16 – "And he answered, Fear not: for they that *be* with us *are* more than they that *be* with them."

Amen

April 4

B irthstones originated in ancient times with the Hebrew priest Aaron's breastplate which held a precious stone for each of the 12 Hebrew tribes.

The tradition continued through various times and peoples until 1912 when the American National Association of Jewelers formed the official list of birthstones we use today. The stones are assigned as follows:

April - Diamond
May - Emerald
June - Pearl
July - Ruby
August - Paridot
September - Sapphire
October - Opal
November - Topaz
December - Turquoise
January - Garnet

February - Amethyst

March - Aquamarine

That is an impressive list, but to those born again, they missed the most precious stone of all - our Lord and Savior, the Rock of our Salvation!

God bless you!

April 5

F ire does not sit still. It moves and spreads. It desperately reaches out all directions seeking oxygen to sustain itself. That is why it's so hard to put out.

Fires in our lives are the same way. They tend to move and spread, especially when we are desperately seeking solutions from any and all sources. That is what makes troubles hard to put out.

It's when we sit still and exalt God that we are able to finally extinguish them.

If things have heated up in your life, and fires continue to spread - be still and wait on God. Pray, praise, and listen, and He will put them out.

Psalm 46:10 – "Be still, and know that I *am* God: I will be exalted among the heathen, I will be exalted in the earth."

Amen

April 6

Sometimes it takes up to two days for a chick to break out of its shell.

Have patience. Work hard at it, but if whatever you're trying to accomplish doesn't happen today, try again tomorrow.

Something will hatch soon.

April 7

Frozen waterfalls freeze over for part of the year, but when the season changes and things warm up, they flow the same way they used to flow.

We, too, go through seasons when things freeze up and stop flowing the way they used to flow; but when our season returns and things warm up, they start flowing again just like they did before.

Such is life. It's not a free fall, but a waterfall that sometimes freezes up; but if you trust God and wait on it, it will start to flow again.

April 8

*P*uffins are birds that can fly underwater.

God has given them power to do what birds do (fly) in any and every situation.

Christians are people that can love while being hated.

God has given us the power to do what Believers do (love one another) in any and every situation.

So love one another, no matter what the situation. You have the power inside you to do so.

April 9

*G*od is not good to me because I am good. God is good to me because He is good.

That is grace and that is good to me.

April 10

Some species of moths never eat anything as adults because they don't have mouths. They have to rely on the energy they have stored from the food they ate as caterpillars.

With that type of life, no wonder they are drawn to the fire.

Some adults are not blessed because they haven't opened their mouths and prayed since they were children.

With that type of life, no wonder they are drawn to the hellfire.

April 11

*G*enesis 1:1 – "In the beginning God created the heaven and the earth. And the earth was without form, and void..."

In the beginning there was nothing. Then God made something out of nothing. The world was chaotic and without form, then God gave it form and created order.

If it's beginning to seem like there is nothing you can do about a situation, and life appears chaotic and things out of shape.

Know that God can change all that. He can make something you need out of nothing. He can put things back in order. He can shape things up.

Trust and believe in God. Rise and praise His Holy Name. This is your new day. This is the beginning.

Amen

April 12

*N*o matter what happens today, you can overcome it through Jesus Christ. He has overcome all things - even death itself - and has given you the same power that strengthened Him in life and raised Him from the dead: the power of the Holy Spirit.

John 16:33 – "These things I have spoken unto you, that in me ye might have peace. In the world ye shall have tribulation: but be of good cheer; I have overcome the world."

Knowing and believing this, have a blessed and peaceful day in the Lord.

Amen

HAPPY *Sunday!*

April 13

*E*ars not only help you hear, but also help you with balance.

That's true in a spiritual sense, too:

Luke 11:38 – "...blessed *are* they that hear the word of God, and keep it."

That's why those who have an ear for God and listen to His commands live such fruitful and balanced lives.

Amen

April 14

*T*he ear continues to hear sound even as you sleep.

Knowing this, rest in the Lord today as you listen to every Word He says.

April 15

The peace of God is beyond our understanding. That is where faith in comes in. It bridges the gap to peace.

Cross that bridge and have a peaceful day.

God bless you.

April 16

If the situation you're in is not comfortable and doesn't appear to fit you, it's probably because you don't belong in it.

So here's a general rule of thumb: if you can't fit all the way in, consider getting all the way out.

HAPPY *Sunday!*

April 17

*G*uesses, rumors, coincidences, appearances, and hunches do not lead to answers nor are answers behind them.

Answers follow questions and questions lead to answers. If you want to know something - ask. If the truth doesn't follow your question, your question will lead you to it.

Seek knowledge, don't try to create it.

Have a blessed day.

April 18

*H*earing the word of God is the first step to being born again.

Romans 10:17 - So then faith cometh by hearing, and hearing by the word of God.

Now that's an earful. I hope you hear me.

April 19

*T*he Lord can bless you in any direction He sends you. Don't think you have to follow in someone else's footsteps or take the same path as those before you in order to be blessed.

Genesis 12:1, 2 - Now the LORD had said unto Abram, Get thee out of thy country, and from thy kindred, and from thy father's house, unto a land that I will shew thee: And I will make of thee a great nation, and I will bless thee...

Genesis 31:3 - And the LORD said unto Jacob, Return unto the land of thy fathers, and to thy kindred; and I will be with thee.

Your blessings are where God leads you, which is not always the way others have been led.

April 20

$\mathscr{N}$othing can or will ever happen that God cannot fix, heal, or restore.

April 21

$\mathscr{H}$ave you ever seen a love that was created and fenced in by the imperfections of the two God brought together?

Love is amazing just like God.

God is love.

Love you!

April 22

*D*on't sit in a hot situation too long because everyone has a boiling point; the point at which things that used to be cool start to bubble up; the point at which you start steaming; the point when your patience begins to evaporate.

Remove yourself, before everything melts down; while you still have a handle on things.

April 23

Anger, envy, hate, violence, cursing and the such are all strings. They can attach to you in different ways and pull you in concerted directions that entertain others when purposefully and artfully done.

Like the strings of puppeteers when working their puppets.

Don't let a puppeteer pull your strings and play you like a puppet today. You're not here to entertain others, and you are no puppet.

April 24

*I*magine going to a store without any money and seeing something you want but don't have any money to purchase. As a matter of fact, you're broke.

Now imagine the store owner going into His own pocket and giving you money to buy that something.

That is what God does in Jesus. We want to eternal life but can't pay the cost ourselves because we have spent all our lives in sin. As a matter of fact, we're broken.

But God reached inside Himself, gave us Jesus, and put Him inside of us. Having suddenly found change, we can now pay the cost of eternal life (acceptance of Jesus as Lord) and obtain all God has in store for us.

Go ahead; purchase what you want with the Blood. Enjoy the unlimited riches you have in Jesus and have a blessed day!

April 25

*J*esus' greatest sermon wasn't on the Mount where He physically stood at His highest. His greatest sermon was on the cross, where He spiritually hung at His lowest.

It's the same in our lives. The high points in life where we speak about different blessings are not our greatest witness. Our greatest witness occurs at the low points where we trust God through troubles and curses.

God bless you!

April 26

$\mathcal{P}$op quizzes can be unfair because you don't see them coming and have no time to prepare.

God doesn't give us pop quizzes. He gives us tests.

He has told us that life is short and full of trouble. He has told us to study and show ourselves approved in the knowledge of His Word. He has told us He will try our hearts.

So don't act surprised when tested. He didn't just pop it on you.

Be prepared. Read, study, learn the Word, and ace the tests you face.

April 27

*S*ome things look right until they start to go left:

Proverbs 16:25—There is a way that seemeth right unto a man, but the end thereof are the ways of death.

It's possible to think you live right and be dead wrong.

Consider the end result of everything you do before you start to do it.

April 28

I am perfect in Christ.

Now, if I could only stay perfectly in Him...

"O wretched man that I am! who shall deliver me from the body of this death?"

(Paul's inference to the saving grace of God in Christ Jesus when lamenting his imperfection...Romans 7:24)

HAPPY *Sunday!*

April 29

*B*aby shampoo prevents stinging that causes tears because it has less of the active cleaning ingredients (surface acting agents – surfactants for short) found in adult shampoo.

While it prevents tearing, it also doesn't get the baby's hair as clean as it would be using an adult shampoo.

Faith in Jesus Christ is adult shampoo. It includes some tears, but it cleanses you completely from all sin.

Everything else is baby shampoo.

In an attempt to avoid life's tears, you can wash with them, but they won't clean you like Jesus—which is something to really cry

April 30

a poor widow was once told to feed God's prophet Elijah with the little food she and her son had left, even before feeding her son and herself.

The woman was obedient and God miraculously sustained her, her son, and the prophet.

In our lives, whether we have a little or a lot, when we obediently put the things of God first—things like love, faith, and hope—God sustains us and these things in our lives.

So put the things of God first. That is how you and those things will last.

God bless you!

May 1

*W*hen Moses walked up to the Red Sea with the Egyptians behind, he had no idea the sea would open.

He just trusted God would do something. In reward of his trust and obedience, God created an opening and parted the sea.

In our lives, we, too, must learn to leave negative things behind us, trust God and go forward in Christ, even into things where we don't see openings, and through situations we don't see how we'll get through.

When we do this, the reward for our trust and obedience is the same. God will create openings where they weren't seen and help us get through things we couldn't see our way through.

Trust God and He will make a way out of no way, just like He did for Moses.

May 2

*A*lways think at least Cross-high of yourself because that is highly Jesus was thinking of you when He gave His life for yours.

Anything else is beneath you and His sacrifice.

May 3

*A*s children of God, when the world gives us trouble, God takes it and passes it right back to the worldly, in whom's hands it rightfully belongs:

Proverbs 8:11 NIV - The righteous person is rescued from trouble, and it falls on the wicked instead.

So if you get into trouble today, put it in God's hands and He'll pass it to where it belongs.

Peace & Blessings!

May 4

*N*o matter what we hold onto or how firm our stance, wind is strong enough to knock us down and blow us away, yet we cannot see it.

Likewise, if we don't honor and stand for God, no matter how firm our stance in the things we have, God is strong enough to knock us down and blow it all away, yet not everyone can see that, either.

Don't be blown away with things. Honor and stand for God.

May 5

*B*e wise about where you put your trust. Some things and people look like they have you covered like an umbrella—until an actual storm arises.

Then, like a cheap umbrella, they seem to turn inside out, and it's hard to get (or keep) a hold them.

Put your trust in God, not people.

May 6

*P*eople can love people. People can also love things. Sometimes people get people and things confused— purposefully or not.

So make sure when someone says they love you, they are not confused and talking about your things.

It happens.

May 7

When someone asks you to weigh in on a situation, no matter how much the truth hurts, put it on the scale. Things will balance out in the end.

Anything else is cheating them out of the truth about what's weighing them down:

A false balance is an abomination to the LORD: but a just weight is His delight.

Be honest - in ALL your dealings.

Amen

May 8

*U*sually, when people speak, the first person that talks is the one to which we listen.

When God said, "Let there be light," He was the first to talk (in our world).

So when looking for answers to questions about things in this world, and others begin to give their take on it, listen to God first.

May 9

*G*od told the nation of Israel that He would give them victory over the city of Ai, but they were not to take any spoils from the city after the battle. The warrior Achan ignored God's command and took riches which He then hid under his tent.

Because of His disobedience, Achan, his entire family, and everything they had were destroyed by fire.

In our lives, when God gives us victory battles with our enemies or the situations that confront us, we should only take away from it the things God allows us to take, things like joy, peace, comfort, restoration, and such. Things like pride, revenge, the desire to taunt, or ridicule for the people or things God has allowed us to defeat should be left behind in the battle.

The victories in our lives are purposed to glorify God and strengthen our belief and faith, not glorify ourselves and impress others.

This is why we sometimes still feel discomfort, and things continue to heat up after we've supposedly resolved troubles - because of the things outside of God's battle plans that we hide in our hearts and plant in our minds.

So to prevent winning the victory and still going through the fire, follow God's battle plans to the letter; remembering that the victory is yours, but the battle and glory is His.

May 10

*T*he thought is unpalatable but please take a moment to ponder it:

Tomorrow, someone somewhere will be wishing they had told someone else that they loved them today.

Life is too short and unpredictable to let anger, division, and strife separate you from those God has given you to love.

Tell someone you love them today, have no regrets tomorrow.

May 11

*E*ven demons know Jesus is Lord; because of this, they fear and tremble.

Remember that when dealing with evil people; understanding that it's what's inside them which makes them so shaky.

May 12

*I*f you don't keep your eyes on the things in front of you, you can stumble over them.

If you keep your eyes on the things behind you, you can stumble over them, too.

Look ahead and stay in stride with the good things God has put before you.

May 13

*R*esponding to every negative thing anyone has to say about you is akin to trying to catch or block every raindrop falling on you in a rainstorm.

Instead of taking on that futile endeavor, let up an umbrella – love – which covers all sins.

May 14

The force of a wrecking ball is found in moving it from under the lifting crane. The more wildly it swings, the more wrecking force it has.

However, it loses all of its wrecking power when it stops moving and is at rest under the crane.

That is when it can be lifted without causing damage to surrounding structures.

Likewise, when we are not at rest under the hand of God, our lives become wrecking balls. So:

"Humble yourselves therefore under the mighty hand of God, and in due time, that He will exalt you."

(First letter from Peter to believers, fifth chapter, sixth verse)

Amen

May 15

$\mathcal{I}$t's not about where you're from, or even where you've been; it's about where you don't go:

Psalm 1:1, 2 – "Blessed is the man that walketh not in the counsel of the ungodly, nor standeth in the way of sinners, nor sitteth in the seat of the scornful."

Walk with God, stand for God, sit and wait on God. That's where your blessing is. That's the place to go and be.

May 16

Rumors tend to run rampant, so when you hear something that you don't know for yourself to be true, don't take it for what it is on surface, always dig a little deeper into the dirt you hear.

That way, if it's not true you'll have some soil to bury the gossip.

Run and tell that.

May 17

The devil wants you to exchange the treasure you have in Christ for his currency of sin so that you'll buy into his lies.

May 18

a s a boy, King David was sent by his father to nourish the frontline soldiers fighting to deliver his nation. The end result of David's obedience to this small assignment was victory over the biggest enemy he had ever seen or faced—Goliath.

Today, God our Father, sends us out to nourish those on the front lines of our lives (relatives and friends) with the love for them He has placed in our hearts.

Be obedient in these small assignments. It is during these times that we, too, face and overcome the biggest enemies and obstacles in our lives.

The Lord works in mysterious ways.

HAPPY *Sunday!*

May 19

*T*he ancient Israelites believed the "reins" (kidney area) or what we call today "guts" were the center of emotions, so they often prayed that God would hold their reins.

Likewise, if we have trusted God to hold our reins, we should trust our instincts and "gut feelings."

So listen to your gut today.

May 20

*W*hen holding a gun, avoid carrying it with your finger on the trigger. This prevents you from accidentally pulling it and making the gun go off.

Likewise, evil thoughts trigger evil actions. So avoid carrying them in your mind. This prevents you from doing them, or trying to pull them off.

But if you think on good things, you'll do good things—the Spirit will pull them off.

Pow!

May 21

$\mathcal{S}$ome packages are so hard to open that I quit buying them and purchase other brands that are easier to open.

Applying this to our lives, if someone has stopped buying into the relationship you have with them, perhaps it was difficult getting you to open up.

Try opening up easier. It shouldn't be so difficult to get things (like love and support) out of you.

If they don't buy it and still go shopping for someone else - it may be that they just don't have any brand loyalty.

Shelve this in prayer!

May 22

Because of its orbit and around the Sun and the constant expansion of the Universe (Hubble's Law), Earth is not in the same position as it was yesterday, and will never be in that position again.

Neither are you.

Today is a new day. As a creature in God's creation, follow the lead of all He created. Put everything from the past behind you and enjoy the new space into which the design and purposes of God have moved you.

Keep revolving around the Son, keep moving, and keep expanding.

It's a new day and things are different.

May 23

*O*nly surrender to God.
You have the victory over everything else.

May 24

*W*ho knows who is bad or good. People can be deceiving—so don't watch out for bad people. Watch out for bad things, like hate, gossip, envy, and the such, because bad people are found in bad things; which is how you know they're bad people:

Ephesians 4:14 – "...whereby they lie in wait to deceive..."

And when watching for bad things, make sure you don't find yourself in them.

May 25

*T*he word Satan means accuser. Satan is known to entice man to disobey God and then turn around and accuse man before God. Satan is also known as the serpent. Serpents have special jaws that allow them to stretch wide open.

End of story.

Moral of the story: Don't let the serpent talk you into anything because after it's done you'll find he has a big mouth.

May 26

*D*on't send your mind where the body of Christ doesn't fit.

Sometimes we go through things because we are trying to go through things that weren't made for us to try to go through.

HAPPY *Sunday!*

May 27

*W*hen a person isn't sure of directions, they look for signs. However, when they know where they're going, signs aren't that important.

They still provide assurance, but the person goes ahead—with or without them.

It's the same with faith. When a person has weak faith, they look for signs. However, when a person has strong faith, signs aren't that important.

They still provide assurance, but strong faith goes on—with or without them.

Have faith. Strong faith.

May 28

*I*f a flying bird faces the wind the right way, the wind goes past it and lifts it up.

If a flying bird does not face the wind the right way, the wind pushes it down.

People are like wind.

If you face them the right way, they'll get past what you've done, or what you're doing, and support you.

If you don't face them the right way, they won't get past what you've done, or doing, and they'll say and do things that bring you down.

Like birds, God has given us the ability to soar, but only when we face people and things the right way.

May 29

*J*esus was once awakened to a troubling storm at sea. His first action was to calm the wind, the cause of the storm.

To restore peace in troubled times, follow His example: address the cause of the storm—not just the effects.

May 31

*Y*ou're a winner!

Waking up is the trophy.

Praise God and take a victory lap around this blessed day in His name!

June 1

*Y*ou're a winner!

Waking up is the trophy.

Praise God and take a victory lap around this blessed day in His name!

June 2

*N*o matter what you're battling, never miss an opportunity to do something good because regardless of what's warring against you - the victory lies in showing love to others.

That's how soldiers in God's army fight.

June 3

*S*ome flowers protect themselves by covering themselves with thorns in areas that they don't want you to touch, like the stems or leaves.

So if pricked by an uncomely response on a subject you approached, recognize that the sharp reaction may be stemming from you touching upon something that they don't want you to touch.

June 4

*W*ater towers are tall and are often placed on high ground in order to provide sufficient pressure to deliver water to homes in case of an emergency. Scientists estimate that each foot of a water tower's height provides a little less than half a pound per square inch of pressure.

The higher the water is kept, the stronger the force of the water as it enters into homes.

Spiritually, water represents the Word of God. The higher we place the Word in our lives, and the more Word we place on top of the Word we already know, the stronger its force when we face trouble and emergencies in our homes.

So keep the Word high and stacked in your life, just like a water tower.

June 5

*F*ire changes color based on the intake of oxygen. In a similar manner, our lives change color based upon our intake of God's Word and our faith in His promises.

If you're not getting enough Word, this may be why you feel blue, turn green with envy, get red with rage, and become yellow with fear, so frequently and so easily. Just a thought.

Let that burn in your mind for a minute.

June 6

A penguin may not have the type of wings it takes to soar high like Eagles, but the wings they do have are perfect at accomplishing the tasks that are most important at their level.

Your gift may not rise to the heights and attention in spaces where others soar, but trust that it is accomplishing what it's meant to accomplish on whatever level it operates.

June 7

K now why you're still here despite all the self-destructive behavior?

Because God didn't design you to give up or be defeated that easily. You're greater than the devices the devil uses in his attempts to destroy you.

So today, no matter what troubles you face, know that you're built to survive them.

1 John 4:4 – " are of God, little children, and have overcome them: because greater is he that is in you, than he that is in the world."

Amen

HAPPY *Sunday!*

June 8

*N*o more fight left in you?

Good.

When the fight is in you, you can't win, but when it's no longer in you, God fights for you, and that's when you win, because God can't lose and learn the battle is His.

That's a win-win situation, so—whatever it is—give to God because you have nothing to lose.

June 9

$\mathcal{G}$od can see you through the darkest hour just as well as He can see you through your brightest moments.

There is no change in His faithfulness or the view He has of you, no matter what you're facing or what you're going through; likewise, there should be no change in your faithfulness or view of Him as an awesome and mighty God.

So whatever you're going through, go through it with God because He is going through with you.

Psalm 139:12 - "Yea, the darkness hideth not from thee; but the night shineth as the day: the darkness and the light are both alike to thee."

June 10

*M*ichael Collins, an astronaut who took a photo of the world from space in 1969, is the only human, alive or dead that wasn't in his picture.

We, too, can sometimes distance and exclude ourselves from the sin and evil around us; having self-righteously elevated ourselves so much higher than everyone else that we begin to lose sight of our own failures and short-comings.

Think about this, and if you see a world of sin without you in it, come back down to Earth and find Jesus. We all sin, but when we believe on Him, He atones for it.

Peace & Blessings (from here to the moon and back)

June 11

*L*ightning builds up in the heavens before it strikes. So does God's wrath.

Romans 2:5 – "But because of your hard and unrepentant heart, you are storing up wrath against yourself for the day of wrath, when God's righteous judgment will be revealed."

June 12

a pot of water on a hot stove will keep things cooking until the water boils away, then a fire starts.

So always make sure there is water in the pot.

Now think of water as the Word of God, and the pot as your life.

As long as the Word is in your life, things are cooking, but if you allow the Word to evaporate, that's when the fires in life start.

So always make sure there is Word in your life.

June 13

*K*eys open doors. If you put your keys on a ring, and the ring is in your pocket, you won't lose your keys.

Faith opens doors. If you put your faith in God, and God is in your heart, you won't lose your faith.

The key is to keep your faith in a safe place – God; doing so will open doors for you that no man can close.

June 14

*T*hings that live in the water don't like to be rained upon.

A water habitat and water falling are not one and the same.

Likewise, people who are poor don't like to be treated poorly.

Poor living and poor treatment are not one and the same. One can learn to live with being poor, but one shouldn't have to live with being treated poorly.

Don't treat others poorly, and don't accept poor treatment, either. Each one of us has riches in Christ Jesus, and God has more for us all.

HAPPY *Sunday!*

June 15

*H*appiness isn't found in just any old stuff— it's found in stuff that makes a difference. Stuff like love, peace, and forgiveness. The kind of stuff you find in Christ.

But hey, I'm just talking stuff.

June 16

*I*f I were following a bus full of friends and you asked me who was so following, I would not name every one of my friends on the bus and say I was following each of them. I would simply respond that I am following the bus. The bus contains all that I am following in it.

God says to love Him and love one another. So don't tell me all the individual things I should or should not be doing in order to be obedient to God. I'll simply Love Him and love you. That contains all the things I should and should not do in it.

June 17

Prayer is not about letting everyone see that you are talking to God. It's about letting God see you are talking to Him. When you open the door on your prayer, you're actually shutting the door on your prayer:

Matthew 6:6 – "But thou, when thou prayest, enter into thy closet, and when thou hast shut thy door, pray to thy Father which is in secret; and thy Father which seeth in secret shall reward thee openly."

So close the door and pray, then Watch God open new doors when you're done.

Amen

June 18

If a pregnant woman suffers organ damage during pregnancy, the unborn child will send stem cells to help repair the damage.

We were born with an instinct to care for our parents. Never lose it.

God had a plan for Joseph, yet he was sold into slavery by his brothers and falsely imprisoned before God exalted him above his brothers and into to the highest position under Pharaoh.

Joseph maintained his character, faith and love for God through all his troubles.

You, too, may be under attack by those you love and trust most.

They may be selling you out and tying you to repented sins and corrected errors.

If so, maintain your character, faith, and love for God throughout all your troubles, then God—who is the same yesterday, today and forever—will deliver and exalt you, too!

June 20

If you look up in the midst of trees, you'll see their covering.

If you look up in the midst of problems, you'll see your covering.

Look up. Jesus has you covered.

June 21

*N*o matter what you've lost—a friend, money, time, a love, a job, your innocence, your reputation, even if it feels like your losing your mind—if you've found God, you're still winning:

Romans 8:37 – "Nay, in all these things we are more than conquerors through him that loved us."

Nothing can separate us from the love of God in Christ Jesus. Not one single thing.

Remember that today.

Amen

June 22

*W*hen you spit gum out in the streets, birds think it's bread and swallow it up. When they do this, the gum gets stuck in their throats and preventing them from drinking or eating. They end up dying a painful, slow death, hungering for the food they thought they had already found.

When nonbelievers spit out nonsense for others to chew on, like "there is no God" or "Jesus is not our Savior," other nonbelievers hear it and it's gets stuck in their minds, preventing them from being nourished by the Truth of the Gospel. They end up dying an eternally painful death, hungering for the truth they thought they had already found.

Don't spit gum out in the streets. It's lethal.

Don't spit lies out about God in the streets.

It's lethal.

HAPPY *Sunday!*

June 23

*L*ooking at one thing through another thing can make one thing seem like it's inside of another thing—even though it is not.

Likewise, looking for happiness through sinful means can make happiness seem like it can be found through sinful means—even though it cannot.

June 24

*I*n hindsight, we see that Jesus was put in a borrowed tomb because death would only hold him long enough to glorify God. He would be coming out of it soon. He is the Son of God.

Now, in faith and foresight, we see that any dead situations we are in don't belong to us, either. We know that we will only be in them long enough to glorify God. We will be coming out of them soon. We are the children of God.

1 Peter 5:10 –"But the God of all grace, who hath called us unto his eternal glory by Christ Jesus, after that ye have suffered a while, make you perfect, stablish, strengthen, settle you."

Amen

June 25

*G*od doesn't make the same day over and over again. Each one He creates is renewed in His mercy and grace.

So don't get up expecting the same old thing. Expect things to change and God to do a new thing:

Isaiah 43:19 – "Behold, I will do a new thing; now it shall spring forth; shall ye not know it? I will even make a way in the wilderness, and rivers in the desert."

Lamentations 3:22,23: "It is of the LORD'S mercies that we are not consumed, because his compassions fail not. They are new every morning: great is thy faithfulness."

So rise up in hope and faith and look for the Lord to do new and good things for you today!

June 26

*a*ntibodies help white blood cells attack germs. If the body comes across germs it has no antibodies for, it quickly creates them and uses memory cells to store the antibodies in case the germs are seen again.

This is call acquired immunity and, loosely speaking, that is how a vaccine works.

Believers use the Word of God to help attack sin and trouble. When we come across sins or trials that threaten to overtake us, we pray and search the scriptures for more wisdom and understanding to overcome these challenges.

If and when we face these challenges again, or see others facing the same obstacles, the Holy Spirit brings us into remembrance of the Truth we used to solve our problems before, allowing us to quickly re-apply it or share it with others.

This is called sanctification and, loosely speaking, that is how self-edification and brotherly love work.

So if you're feeling a little sin-sick or you're risen with Christ but feeling like you might be coming down with something, get a dose of The Word and strengthen your immune system—there are a lot of things going around out there!

June 27

$\mathcal{G}$od and I are workout partners. Each morning, as God lifts the Sun, I lift the Son.

Try a few reps. It keeps you strong in the Lord – making it easy to lift others – as God continues to brighten your day.

$\mathcal{E}$ver try to lift something and couldn't, or worse, hurt yourself trying?

Try bending your knees and lifting heavy objects with your legs.

Ever try to solve a problem and couldn't, or made it worse?

Try bending your knees (in prayer) and lifting heavy burdens with your faith.

Both avoid injuries and ease the lifting!

1 Thessalonians 5:17 – "Pray without ceasing."

June 29

*W*hen nothing is right, it's difficult to explain what's wrong. That's what we have the Spirit for, and that's when He does the talking:

Romans 8:26 – "...the Spirit helps us in our weakness. We do not know what we ought to pray for, but the Spirit himself intercedes for us through wordless groans."

So talk to God, even when you can't - He'll help you get it out.

June 30

*I*t's not the material that makes a nice outfit stand out—it's the pattern.

Likewise, acts of righteousness can be found immaterial if they aren't the norm. It's a pattern of righteousness that God is seeking and that's what will make you stand out:

Titus 2:7 – "In all things shewing thyself a pattern of good works..."

Amen

July 1

*R*oads may dip, rise, twist and turn but they're designed to lead to a destination.

In life there are ups and downs, strange twists, and sudden turns, but every journey has a destination.

Believers have been predestined to eternal life in Christ. Heaven is our destination.

In our hearts and minds, any other road is a dead end.

Map things out in your heart and mind today. Where are you headed?

July 2

$\mathcal{T}$he bible tells of seven brothers who attempted to perform an exorcism without having a relationship with Jesus and the power of the Holy Spirit.

The demon knew Jesus, but had never heard of the brothers and apparently sensed their lack of power. He then began to beat and disrobe them until they fled naked in shame.

Life without Jesus and Holy Ghost power is an epic fail. Situations can beat you down and strip you of the hope and energy to go forward.

Introduce yourself as a Child of the King to every situation you face. You already know Satan's name and character. Make sure he knows yours (in Christ)!

July 3

*J*esus cleaned the unclean, loved the un-loved, washed the unwashed, saved the unsaved, forgave the unforgiven, made holy the unholy, and made Godly the ungodly.

How? All things are possible with God.

So with that understanding—think the unthinkable, do the undoable, believe the unbelievable, achieve the unachievable, and reach the unreachable.

The bar has been set high—but you can reach it in Christ!

July 4

*J*acob wrestled with God all night long. When he submitted, it changed his life and his walk forever.

God is the same yesterday, today and forever. As such, He is still wrestling with Believers today.

He won't twist our arms but He has several submission holds—the most persuasive being the Head(of my life)lock. First he puts your hands together and gets you on your knees. Then He gets His arms around you, turns you, and faces you in a new direction where all you can see is up.

After all that, if you still haven't tapped out of sin, He frees you with a Three-count (Father, Son, Holy Ghost)!

July 5

*I*f you can imagine confession of sin as a washing machine, then consider repentance of sin the dryer.

Psalm 28:13 – "He that covereth his sins shall not prosper: but whoso confesseth and forsaketh them shall have mercy."

So when you confess to God about something you have done wrong, stop doing it.

Anything less will leave you unclean, and make you repeat the cycle.

July 6

Shoes don't elevate by themselves—they need feet inside them to do that.

People don't elevate by themselves—they need God inside them to do that.

Psalm 75:6 – "For promotion cometh neither from the east, nor from the west, nor from the south. But God is the judge: he putteth down one, and setteth up another."

To whatever or wherever you're trying rise, leap for it with God inside.

SCAN ME

July 7

Keep your eyes on what the Lord has ahead, not on what the devil caused behind. If you want to see joy in your life, look to the writer of it, not the eraser of it.

Hebrews 12/2 – "Looking unto Jesus the author and finisher of our faith; who for the joy that was set before him endured the cross, despising the shame, and is set down at the right hand of the throne of God."

Amen

July 8

*M*ost standard combination locks have three numbers or symbols you select to unlock and access things that are locked away.

Sound familiar? Of course it does. God has peace, joy and eternal life locked in Christ - open to all who believe.

So unlock an abundant life in Christ using the ultimate combination—The Father, The Son, and The Holy Spirit!

God bless you!

July 9

*W*hen buying a new car, you don't just pick it out and take it home. You test drive it.

You check under the hood and inspect the engine. You check the tires. You test drive the vehicle. You take the car uphill and downhill. You test its ability to turn and handle curves. You evaluate its performance at high and low speeds, on highways and streets. Then you make the decision to take the car home or leave it on the lot for the next buyer.

Believers go through a similar inspection process.

God doesn't just listen to our words, He examines our hearts. He looks at our walk. He tests our faith and belief. He takes us over the highest mountains and through the lowest valleys. He evaluates how we turn away from evil and sin. He checks our performance when things are moving, when things have stopped, and when things are idle. He checks how we handle ourselves in the streets, and when we trip (and fall). At the end of our test drive, comes Judgment day.

So don't get left on the lot for the next buyer because he's hard on cars and takes them through Hell, where they end up staying forever.

Perform according to your Make(r) and Model (Jesus)—then one day God will take you home!

July 10

In this life there are more airplanes in the ocean than there are submarines in the sky.

That's peculiar.

In the next life, I wonder will there be more hypocritical "saints" in Hell than there are repented sinners in Heaven.

That will be peculiar, too, but it's supposed to be:

1 Peter 2:9 – "But ye *are* a chosen generation, a royal priesthood, an holy nation, a peculiar people..."

Amen

July 11

*S*cientists say the Universe is expanding. Well, Believers already knew that:

Romans 11:33 – "O the depth of the riches both of the wisdom and knowledge of God! How unsearchable *are* his judgments, and his ways past finding out!"

The more you find out about God and His creation, the more you find out there is more to find out.

Scientists—keep searching. Believers—keep believing. God is unsearchable but there is plenty of Space to find Him, when you realize without Him you are lost.

So don't get left on the lot for the next buyer because he's hard on cars and takes them through Hell, where they end up staying forever.

Perform according to your Make(r) and Model (Jesus)—then one day God will take you home!

July 12

*P*art of what it takes to walk away from God is to take part in things that those who don't know God are taking part in; because to take part in things that are not of God takes part of you away from Him, and He requires our all.

Ephesians 5:7 – "Be not ye therefore partakers with them."

Amen

July 13

*F*olks trying to steal your joy and drive you crazy today?

Use your auto-mobility in Christ:

Put the brakes on their nonsense.

Take a detour through love, patience and forgiveness.

Move in the Spirit.

Yield to Jesus.

Take the high road.

Avoid taking their route— they're still under construction.

If things are still headed in the wrong direction, use your GPS (Godly Positioning System) to find another way.

Whatever you do, stay in your lane, keep it moving and, most importantly, remain in your vehicle at all times—don't let anyone run over you!

July 14

*B*ad times are not good times, but sometimes they prepare you for them:

Hebrews 12:11 – "Now no chastening for the present seemeth to be joyous, but grievous: nevertheless afterward it yieldeth the peaceable fruit of righteousness unto them which are exercised thereby."

So go through what you have to go through, knowing it will get you where you need to be.

July 15

*W*hen you no longer have use for some-thing, or it no longer holds value for you, you discard it. However, that does not make it garbage.

It may still hold value to others. It may be able to be recycled and put to other uses—even better ones.

It's the same with former relationships. So don't put down people you once loved, nor belittle those you once esteemed.

Like you, they've changed and moved on to different people and things. That alone does not make them trash.

God bless you and all your friends - old, new, and future!

July 16

C arpenters carry toolboxes. When building or repairing, they search the toolbox for the appropriate tools.

Believers carry Bibles. When building or repairing, we search the Bible for Wisdom and understanding.

Open your toolbox today—build and repair a few things through Christ.

If it's broken, Jesus can fix it— He was and still is a Carpenter!

HAPPY *Sunday!*

July 17

Same God—different day, same blessings - different way.

Lament stations 3:23 – "It is of the LORD'S mercies that we are not consumed, because his compassions fail not. They are new every morning: great is thy faithfulness."

July 18

I love it when science catches up to my faith! A good friend shared the following news article with me:

"Ever walk into a room with a purpose, only to forget what that purpose was? Turns out doors are to blame for these strange memory lapses.

Researchers at a leading university have discovered that passing through a doorway triggers what is known as an event boundary, separating one set of thoughts and memories from the next.

$\mathcal{Y}$our brain files away the thoughts you had in the last room and prepares a clean slate for the next."

I could have told them that and saved them a lot of grant money.

Jesus is the Door to new life. Life through Him provides a clean slate and fresh outlook. Old things pass away and all things are made new.

If you've been born again, and can't remember your past sins, it's not because you're aging—t's The Door!

So the next time you feel like you're losing your mind, thank Jesus because you really are losing it—but it's the old one!

July 19

*W*hen ants reach an impassable point, some will lie down and hold onto others to create a bridge.

We were at an impassable point in sin until Jesus laid down His life for us and bridged the gap between us and God.

Today, you may know someone at an impassible point. As a follower of Christ, you know exactly what to do: lay down your life (sacrifice time and

July 20

*I*n His book of wisdom, God says the righteousness of the perfect shall direct his way: but the wicked shall fall by his own wickedness.

Jesus confirmed in His sermon on the mount that it rains on everyone—the good and the bad.

Because Every Day is "Son"day.

SCAN ME

*I*f you live under the sky, sooner or later it will rain in your life. Rain leaves puddles. Puddles form on uneven landscapes and low ground. However, unlike rain, puddles can be avoided by walking on straight roads and high ground.

It's the same in our spiritual lives. Like rain falling from the sky, sooner or later we have troubles. However, it tends to gather and linger in crooked and lowly behaviors—unrighteousness and sin.

We can limit and avoid the trouble we face by walking with God and taking the high road in life. The path to righteousness is a straight and narrow road. Trouble doesn't last there.

Elevate yourself in Christ and avoid lowly thoughts, words and actions. Walk in faith and love. What gathers there is mercy and truth—

which will linger with you through all eternity!

July 21

$\mathcal{S}$ carab beetles roll away cow dung and lay eggs in them. When the ancient Egyptians saw that young scarab beetles seemed to emerge from the dung balls, they associated them with the Sun which they considered a God and the source of all life.

We still have this type of thinking going on today. There are people who associate messy situations and circumstances with life and good times. As such, they seek to start and live in messy situations. Lying, backstabbing, gossiping, and the like, seem to be their source of life.

Currents are movements of water carried by tides, wind, or differences in temperature or salt content. Currents move water from one part of the ocean to another and between the top and bottom.

Waves are not currents. Waves are energy moving through the water but they don't move the water very far.

True worship of our Father in Heaven is like a current. It's carried by faith, hope, and love: faith in Jesus, hope for the completion of his will and purposes in our lives, and love for God and one another.

True worship can carry us from glory to glory and we travel through the ups and downs of life.

False worship is like a wave. It's worship based upon temporal material blessings and self-righteousness. It energizes momentarily but does not get us far, and mostly leaves us down and out.

So now that you can recognize the difference, stop making waves and move in true worship. It will keep your salvation current and will move it into eternity.

July 23

*L*eaky faucets are annoying. They're messy and run on for no reason. Worst of all, they waste water they should be holding to satisfy someone's thirst.

When I see or hear one running, I call a plumber to fix it—to make it stop.

Leaky people are annoying, too. They're messy and run on and on about others for no good reason. Worst of all, they waste love they should be holding to satisfy someone's thirst.

When I hear someone running on and on about people, I pray and ask God to fix them—to make them stop.

Let's not say mean and hurtful things about one another.

Let's love one another, and satisfy each other's thirst.

HAPPY *Sunday!*

July 24

G ears, or cogs, are rotating machine parts with teeth that mesh with similar parts in order to turn objects and transmit power. Gears transmit power in automobiles, hence the term auto transmission. They are used in other mechanical objects to change direction or motion.

When a car is idled and in neutral, you can switch gears and move it. When you need a mechanical object to change functions, you can switch gears and give it a new purpose.

The Word of God can be used in the same fashion. Scripture meshes with other scripture to churn truth and transmit the power of God to Believers.

The Word transmits power to deliver you from evil and make you whole. It can be

used to turn you around and guide you into all righteousness. It can be used to change your motion, making you swift to hear, slow to speak, and slow to wrath.

The devil is liar! Don't let him strip your gears! You are more than just another cog in the machine—you're a child of The Most High God.

So if you're stalled, stuck in neutral, or headed in the wrong way—get into gear with The Word!

HAPPY *Sunday!*

July 25

a s believers, God says we're the head and not the tail.

The head uses Godly wisdom to get out of mess. The tail wags and spreads mess.

The head uses Godly understanding to avoid mess. The tail foolishly sits in mess.

The head confesses sin and is forgiven for mess. The tail keeps pointing until it's stuck in the mess.

So if you are in a mess, don't spread it or sit in it. Make God the head of your life, and He'll get your tail out of it!

July 26

Sugar-pie.
Honey-bun.
Sweetheart.
Sweetie-pie.
Candy man.
Candy girl.
Cupcake.
Muffin.
Pudding.

I could go on and on but Jesus will always be the sweetest name I know!

HAPPY *Sunday!*

July 27

*D*avid fought his battle against Goliath in the name of The Lord.

A name represents character. David went into battle maintaining a Godly character. This (and the rock he carried) was the cornerstone of his victory.

In our lives, we, too, must maintain a Godly character in spiritual battles. The Lord is our Rock and the Cornerstone of our faith. His name is a strong tower that stores righteous weapons such as faith and hope.

When we envelope ourselves in His righteous character, we strengthen ourselves and our position against enemies.

So whatever giant you're facing today, face it in faith, face it with hope, and face it in the name of the LORD—the Rock and Cornerstone of your victory!

July 28

*S*ometimes you may feel as if your dreams and hopes are illegitimate. You might even consider giving up on them and putting them away.

That is exactly how a man named Joseph felt when he discovered his fiancée, Mary, was pregnant before they had consummated their union. He thought about quietly canceling their wedding plans until an angel told him that the baby was not illegitimate, but born of God's Holy Spirit.

The angel told Joseph to go ahead and marry his fiancée. Joseph followed the angel's instruction and the union brought forth the greatest blessing the world has ever known - Jesus Christ.

So don't give up on any of the dreams God has planted in you, no matter how illegitimate they may appear. God can bless you above all you can ask or imagine, regardless of how things seem.

*I*f He put it in you, to His glory, He'll pull it out of you. After all, He promised to complete every good work He begins in you.

So trust in God and don't ever give up—no matter how things look.

July 29

*G*od says an inheritance gained too soon will not be blessed.

As a believer and joint-heir with Christ, there are wonderful and amazing things coming your way—today and forever. Don't rush them.

Have faith and patience. Walk WITH God, not ahead of Him.

July 30

*W*hen you get a grip on a rubber ball, unless you have it all in your hand, some parts of it will expand and get bigger.

It's the same with problems caused by our sins. If we don't get a grip on the entire problem, the parts we don't a have a handle on will only get bigger and worse.

So don't trust your own hands with the big problems in life. Get a grip on everything you face with the hand of God. His hands are bigger and can completely cover things onto which we can't get a full grip.

Isaiah 48:13 –"...my right hand hath spanned the heavens..."

July 31

*L*ove is the pulse of those alive in Christ.
Check your pulse today. Make sure you're not
dead.

August 1

*H*ares regulate their body temperature
through their ears. When too cold, they con-
strict the blood vessels which retain heat. When
too hot, they expand the vessels which cools
them down. Survival and comfort are found in
their ears, which is why they are so big.

Believers have the same ear for God, which the
blood of Jesus regulates. When things grow cold
or heat up in our lives, The Blood expands and
covers our spirits. Our survival and comfort de-
pend on hearing from God, which is why we
have such big ears for His Word.

God bless you!

Because Every Day is "Son"day.

August 2

*W*hat is the shape of water? It takes on the form of whatever it's poured into.

The Word of God is the same way. It's tailored to fit you and whatever situations you face.

Water moves and expands inside an object until it has filled every open space.

The Word of God does the same inside you.

So talk to God today. He has a fitting message for you. One that will fill every empty area of your life!

God bless you!

August 3

F air exchange is no robbery:

James 5:26— ...pray for one another, that ye may be healed...

I got you. Get me.

August 4

L egal blindness is not total blindness. It is the inability to see objects from 20 feet away, even wearing glasses or contacts that others can see from 200 feet away. People with normal vision (20/20) but less than 20 degrees of side vision (tunnel vision) are also considered legally blind.

Spiritual blindness is not total blindness. It is the inability to clearly see God's purpose and plan for your life, despite the trials, temptations or blessings in front of you. Spiritual blindness also applies to those who only focus on themselves and can't see others around them suffering. Or, when

SCAN ME

in trouble, they can't see that God is standing right by their side.

Don't fret if, based on the aforementioned definitions, you fall into the spiritually blind category. Governments provide special benefits for the legally blind and God provides special benefits for the spiritually blind. The legally blind have social services, Braille, seeing eye dogs and canes; the spiritually blind have worship services, The Bible, pastors to guide them and prayer to help navigate their way.

So don't let this handicap keep you from living an abundant life. Look on the things of others and keep looking to God—even when you can't see Him that well. We all see things dimly now, but one day all things will be clear and God will be as visible to us, as we are to Him. Meanwhile, enjoy His benefits!

God bless you!

August 5

*H*as your cell phone ever dropped a call? Sometimes competing signals overlap and cancel each other out. Other times the cell tower is too far away and the signal is too weak to pick up. These locations are called dead spots.

Fellowship with God and others can be disrupted the same way. Sin is a dead spot with God. Adultery is a dead spot with a spouse. Disloyalty is a dead spot with a friend. Fear and doubt are dead spots with hope and faith.

These types of spiritual locations cancel out the wisdom and blessings God has for us because they are too far away from His will and purpose to produce positive outcomes.

Be mindful of the actions, thoughts and deeds in your current location. You may be canceling out the positive signals you should be receiving.

But if you are dropping calls, don't worry, God is a faithful carrier and the name of The Lord is a strong tower—the righteous can run to Him and find saved messages.

If things have gone dead where you are, keep moving in a righteous direction until you get a clear spiritual signal. God has a message of hope and blessings He's been trying to get through to you!

August 6

C ounting is easy until someone starts saying numbers that are not in sequence with your count. That's when counting becomes hard and confusing. It may feel like the easiest thing to do is to start counting again from the beginning, but that wastes time and you may never reach your final count.

Counting on God is easy, too, until things get out of order and things happen that you didn't count on. That's when counting on God can become difficult or confusing, but don't lose faith. Don't stop counting on Him, because you if you do, you will never receive what He has for you:

Proverbs 3:5 – "Trust in the LORD with all thine heart; and lean not unto thine own understanding."

Count on God today, no matter what sequence of events occurs or what happens out of order.

August 7

G od says if we cast our bread upon the water it will return to us, meaning if we give and have patience, the same things will, in turn and time, be given to us.

However, patience is the key. How many times have we been at the shore and walked away too quickly, leaving bread that arrived soon after we turned for others to come and eat?

Give, and wait:

Luke 6:38 New International Version – "Give, and it will be given to you. A good measure, pressed down, shaken together and running over, will be poured into your lap. For with the measure you use, it will be measured to you."

August 8

*T*he only thing you need on any journey with God is strong faith and courage:

Joshua 1:9 –"Have not I commanded thee? Be strong and of a good courage; be not afraid, neither be thou dismayed: for the LORD thy God *is* with thee whithersoever thou goest".

So before you leave, no matter where you're going, check your baggage and unpack fear and dismay.

August 9

Sometimes the rain in our lives is part of our grooming.

James 1:2 – "My brethren, count it all joy when ye fall into divers temptations; Knowing this, that the trying of your faith worketh patience. But let patience have her perfect work, that ye may be perfect and entire, wanting nothing."

So whatever you're going through, know that things (and you) will look better when it's over.

August 10

According to experts, the average woman loses between 50 and 100 hair strands per day, even up to 150 in some cases. Most of it comes out when brushing and styling the hair. Old, dead, hair is replaced by new growth.

So don't be afraid of brushing because as it removes the dead hair, it facilitates new hair-styles.

The same thing happens when God brushes away the dead things hanging onto us. Every day we lose more and more of our old dead selves, as new growth replaces old behaviors.

So don't be afraid of God's brushing because as it removes the old you, it facilitates a new lifestyle.

August 11

*G*od is aware of evil lurking around us of which we are not aware, and He is protecting us from the hurt and harm it means to cause us.

This is why we should always be thankful, because there are always reasons for which to be thankful, whether we see them and know it, or not.

God is keeping us right now. Let us be thankful.

HAPPY *Sunday!*

August 12

*W*e start developing taste buds in the womb. By the third trimester of pregnancy, babies have more taste buds than they'll have in their entire lives. Studies show that by the time they are born they have developed preferences in flavor based on what they tasted in the womb. When babies eat, their mouths explode with flavor, which is why they are such picky eaters.

If you are a child of God your tastes developed the same way. God says He created us in Christ before the foundation of the world to do good works. He developed a preference in us to believe His Word and live righteously. We were predestined to walk with Him and receive blessings.

So today, no matter which one of the five known tastes the world tries to feed you (salty, bitter, sour, sweet or umami), remember who and what you are in Christ. Taste everything in faith, and you will see that the Lord is good. Your mouth will explode with praise, and you'll love the flavor of His favor!

August 13

A nswering foolishness questions wisdom when the answers are as foolish as the questions:

Proverbs 26:4 – "Answer not a fool according to his folly, lest thou also be like unto him…"

August 14

G od says owe no man nothing but love.

Avoid eternal bankruptcy and cash out on hate, division and strife. Thanks to Jesus you are out of debt, so bless somebody out of the treasures of your new heart!

August 15

*E*ach day you should drink half your body weight in water (200 pounds = 100 ounces). By the time you realize you are thirsty—dry lips, dry throat, urge to drink liquid—you are already dehydrated. However, it's difficult to determine when your body needs water prior to the sensation of thirst. That is why drinking guidelines were created.

God says Believers should be in perpetual prayer and continual praise. If not, by the time you realize you need to get back into the Word and resume a sincere relationship with God (experiencing a dry life, dried up blessings, and having an urge to hear something true) you are usually already facing some severe trial or test. That is why it's so important to maintain a truthful and spiritual relationship with God at all times.

So don't wait until you're thirsting for God's deliverance from hurt, harm or danger to seek His Word. Seek Him early, before you get into trouble. Pray, read and meditate on God's Truth regularly. Weigh your burdens and drink from the Word of God accordingly. A sip or two of His wisdom and understanding each day will keep your soul safe, happy, and well-hydrated in Christ!

August 16

W hen fish sense a disturbance in the water, they instinctively turn in the opposite direction. The tentacled water snake knows this, so when hunting, he positions himself under a fish with his tail at its head and his head at its tail.

Then he moves his tail. When the fish reflexively turns, it swims right into the snake's mouth.

The devil is the same way. He knows those that are weak in faith have a tendency to turn from God at the slightest trial or trouble. That is why he puts obstacles in front of them as they move toward God then devours them whole when they turn and run back to the sin they thought was safely behind them.

So don't turn from God, no matter what obstacle is placed in your way, it's only a trick of the devil.

August 17

*G*od has a way of positioning those who love and trust Him in such a way that their enemies can't reach them:

Psalm 127:7 – "The LORD shall preserve thee from all evil: he shall preserve thy soul."

Once you're in that position, don't move. Just praise God be still.

Amen

August 18

*S*ea cucumbers have bodies that can grow up to three feet long and if cut in three pieces will grow back whole.

Let that encourage all who believe upon the name of Jesus Christ. If your life has been ripped or torn apart by the trying circumstances and seasons of life, trust the goodness of God. Jesus is able to restore and make whole everything that has come apart.

Just trust and believe Him:

John 5:6 – "When Jesus saw him lie, and knew that he had been now a long time in that case, he saith unto him, Wilt thou be made whole?"

August 19

*F*ollowers of Christ are like trees planted and rooted in love. Our fruit is of the Spirit, and we give no shade because we're full of the Light the Son shines through us.

Ephesians 3:15-17 – "For this cause I bow my knees unto the Father of our Lord Jesus Christ, Of whom the whole family in heaven and earth is named, That he would grant you, according to the riches of his glory, to be strengthened with might by his Spirit in the inner man; That Christ may dwell in your hearts by faith; that ye, being rooted and grounded in love..."

August 20

*I*f a starfish loses one or more of its appendages, that does not make it any less a starfish. As a matter of fact, as long as it's central nerve ring is intact, but t can regenerate those limbs and return to its former shape and size.

In our spiritual lives, the Spirit of God regenerates us through the Word of God in the same manner. As long as our faith is intact, Jesus will regenerate and restore every gift that makes us stars in His eyes.

So bless God for His mercy and grace, and have a blessed day—Superstar!

August 21

*O*f the 6000 or so stars visible to the naked eye, about 58 of them have been used by travelers since antiquity to navigate and find direction. This can be done night and day using the Sun and other stars so bright they can be seen during daytime, too. The fixed locations and faithful orbits of the stars make celestial navigation a sure and trusted process.

As Followers of Christ, we use the Word of God to determine our location, direction and paths in life. Jesus is our Bright Morning Star and our Day Star because He shines on us at all times. He is visible in our hearts night and day— good times and bad.

So when you are lost, or aren't quite sure which path to take in a situation—look to Jesus. Follow the road the Word of God tells you take. Ensure you stay the course by regularly checking your location relative to the will of God.

God is faithful and true to His Word. He will do what He said He would do: lead you, guide you, and never forsake you. So keep your eyes on Him and He will show you the way!

HAPPY *Sunday!*

August 22

*T*he best part of the story about the prodigal son is that his father saw him coming home from far off.

That loving father represents our Father in heaven, and no matter how far you have moved away from Him, He is still looking for you, watching, waiting for you to come home.

That's love.

So come home to it.

August 23

W hen you leave God and fall from Grace, you descend into worldly ways like a dead leaf falls in autumn.

Once nestled in sin—like the leaf in the dirt—the wrath of God rakes you into the pile of judgment.

Just like we do piles of fallen and dead leaves, your soul is discarded and burned.

Hold onto God. Never leave Him, because He will never leave you - unless you let go in the Fall.

August 24

*F*lames dance, and when you move with God you learn how to dance around them.

Psalm 30:11 – "Thou hast turned for me my mourning into dancing: thou hast put off my sackcloth, and girded me with gladness;"

August 25

*S*heep trails are crooked because sheep tend to look ahead, to the side, and to the rear when walking. Turning the body to look sideways and backwards adds a slight "wiggle" to their gait that translates to a crooked path of hoof prints. Never maintaining a forward focus, it's no wonder they often wander, get lost, or become prey to predators.

As the Good Shepherd's sheep, we, too, sometimes focus too much on what's happening around us and what's happened in the past.

When we take our focus off God and His will for our lives, it becomes difficult to walk in line with His Word. Time and time again, we lose our way and end up troubled and confused.

We all sin (less and less in Christ), but praise be to God we have a Good Shepherd that will come and find us when we wander away. Thank God we have a Shepherd that will forgive our sins, defend us from our enemies, and shield us from harm!

That's the God I serve! That's the God I love! That's the God I pray blesses, keeps, and shepherds you through this day!

August 26

Balaam, a prophet of Beor, once tried to go in a direction and take actions that God expressly disapproved. However, the donkey on which Balaam rode, saw and heard God's warning along the path and refused to carry the prophet further. Angered, the prophet beat the animal, then something special happened: the donkey spoke. This miracle opened the prophet's eyes to the danger in the path ahead. Balaam got the message and aligned his plans with God's.

In our lives, we sometimes take paths paved with intentions that are contrary to God's will. When we ignore God's will, He often gets our attention by talking to us through the vehicles that carry us. Gods tends to speak to us through finances, family concerns, issues with friends, even problems with our health, to name a few voices. These are languages we understand, even when stubborn.

Because Every Day is "Son" day.

If one of the vehicles in your life is stalled and not moving forward as you hoped it would, don't beat yourself up or give up on it. Examine the path and actions you're taking in that area of life, and make sure you aren't missing God's messages and direction.

HAPPY *Sunday!*

August 27

C rocodiles eat their food whole, so they swallow stones and use them to digest the food in their stomachs. As the stones move and rotate within, they crush the meal that otherwise would be difficult to digest.

As followers of Christ, we put the Word of God (our Rock) in our hearts and minds and use it to break down things we find hard to understand—things that otherwise would be difficult to digest.

August 28

*T*he news is written to help you understand what's happening in the world around you.

The Good News (Gospel means good news) was written to help you understand there is hope despite what is happening in the world around you.

The Gospel gives you extra information. That's why it's extra important you read it:

Romans 15:4 – "For whatsoever things were written aforetime were written for our learning, that we through patience and comfort of the scriptures might have hope."

HAPPY *Sunday!*

August 29

*T*he kind of light you have is the result of the kind of light you use, which is the result of the kind of light you need:

Matthew 13:5 – "But other fell into good ground, and brought forth fruit, some an hundredfold, some sixtyfold, some thirtyfold..."

Whatever type of light it is, praise God for it, and be sure to let it shine.

August 30

SCAN ME

*W*hen Jesus rose from the dead, the disciples did not find an empty grave. Jesus had left the cloth that covered him in death in the tomb.

If you have risen with Christ, make certain you've left the sin that covered you in death in the tomb.

Because Every Day is "Son"day.

August 31

*L*ike one bad apple, it only takes one bad decision to ruin everything else.

Be wise today.

Walk in the love, wisdom, and understanding found in the life and teachings of Jesus.

September 1

*I*t sounds a bit silly and maybe TMI, but salvation is like personalized toilet paper.

If your name is on the roll, it'll wipe away your mess.

Smile and have a blessed day!

September 2

*P*alm trees are remarkable! They survive storms because they are able to bend with the storms—all the way to the ground, if necessary. It's difficult to uproot them because they are so flexible and, unlike most trees, they don't have branches and leaves catching the wind and pulling the trunk. When the storm ends, palm trees straighten up and are stronger and even more flexible than they were before.

As Believers, we are just as remarkable in Christ. We're able to overcome the storms of life by humbling ourselves and bending our knees to the ground in prayer. It's impossible to uproot us because we are planted in Christ and we don't have all the worldly concerns and burdens the people falling to the left and right of us have. The cares of life don't pull us down. We trust God and when our storms end, our faith is stronger, giving us even more power to overcome future obstacles.

Now isn't it easy to see why palm trees are symbols of victory, sun and paradise? If we continue to persevere and maintain our stand as the palm tree does, we'll find ourselves living victoriously, under the Son and in eternal paradise.

Praise God! Bless you!

September 3

A lobster's blood is not red like ours. It has copper in it, which makes it blue. It's the iron that makes our blood red.

Spiritually speaking, a sinners blood is not like ours, either—not the blood of someone who lives in sin. Their blood is as blue as the sky of the world they love.

Our blood is red like Jesus', because He is in our hearts and that makes us His.

September 4

*W*hen you fall, everything you are carrying falls with you.

But when God picks you back up, He picks up everything you dropped, too:

Joel 2:25 - And I will restore to you the years that the locust hath eaten..

Amen

September 5

*Y*ou wouldn't drink out of a filthy cup would you?

Luke 11:39 - And the Lord said unto him, Now do ye Pharisees make clean the outside of the cup and the platter; but your inward part is full of ravening and wickedness.

Neither does the Lord.

September 6

*S*ome people are beautiful—until they open their mouths.

1 Peter 3:3 - Your beauty should not come from outward adornment, such as elaborate hairstyles and the wearing of gold jewelry or fine clothes. Rather, it should be that of your inner self, the unfading beauty of a gentle and quiet spirit, which is of great worth in God's sight.

So keep your heart clean, or keep your mouth shut.

September 7

The address on my license will lead you to a structure in Michigan, but my real home is a building not made by man:

2 Corinthians 5:1 - For we know that if our earthly house of *this* tabernacle were dissolved, we have a building of God, an house not made with hands, eternal in the heavens.

Glory Hallelujah to our God!

September 8

No matter how low or high your station in life, the same things affect us all in the same way:

1 Corinthian 10:13 - There hath no temptation taken you but such as is common to man..

So let's pray for one another, instead of looking up or down at each other. We all need all the help we can get.

Have a blessed day!

September 9

The chuckwalla is a large desert lizard that acts just like a Believer. When threatened by predators, it will run under a rock and inflate the loose folds of skin along its body, making it difficult for the predator to reach it or pull it out. It's the perfect defense.

As followers of Christ, whenever threatened by the devourer, we run to our Rock and fill the loose areas of our lives with the Word of God. We scurry and hide under the crevices of trust and faith and wait on His providence.

Nothing can separate us from the love and care we find in God though Christ Jesus. He is our Perfect Defense, and we are as safe as chuckwallas.

God is amazing!

HAPPY *Sunday!*

September 10

W hen you draw using a pencil that has no eraser, there is no room for mistakes. Yet, we all make mistakes.

Spiritually, the sacrifice of Jesus Christ is the eraser for the pencil we use to draw out lives. None of us are perfect and we have all sinned, but He has erased them.

Believing this gives you a pencil with an eraser.

Not believing this is a mistake that you can't erase.

So believe, then draw out an abundant life and eternal salvation.

September 11

*R*emember this when dealing with difficult people in your life:

You can love your worst enemy, when Jesus is your best friend.

God bless and keep you!

September 12

*T*he cape ground squirrel has a tail so long and bushy, it can actually use it for shade.

I know people like that. They carry their own shade.

Smile and have a blessed day!
#shade #shady #shaded

September 13

$\mathcal{T}$he seed of a plant is in its fruit. Some plants, such as the lodgepole pine, have fruit that is completely covered in thick resin. The fruit cannot release the seed inside until a fire has melted the resin. Often these types of seeds will lay dormant for years until a wildfire awakens them.

In our lives, we can sit for years with unaccomplished goals and unattained dreams; having our sins keeping us dormant. We can be so covered in sin and disobedience to God's will that only a storm strong enough to create a fire in our lives will awaken us.

So don't curse the fire you've been through/you're going through/you'll go through. It is God's way of melting your sins and awakening the seeds He has planted in you, especially the ones that have long been dormant.

God bless you.

September 14

*F*ocusing on worldly concerns blurs the vision God has for you:

2 Corinthians 4:4 - ...the god of this world hath blinded the minds of them which believe not, lest the light of the glorious gospel of Christ, who is the image of God, should shine unto them.

Focus on the things of God, and watch your world clear up.

September 15

*T*hrough the flood, in the storm, and on the darkest of days, trust God because He keeps His promises:

Isaiah 54:10 - For the mountains shall depart, and the hills be removed; but my kindness shall not depart from thee, neither shall the covenant of my peace be removed, saith the LORD that hath mercy on thee. Amen

September 16

*T*he weather in any particular season lags behind the start of the season because it takes the Earth some time to warm up or cool down.

So if God has told you this is a new season in your life, but you don't feel the effects— wait on the Lord. The hot situations will cool down, and things which cooled off will hear back up - in due season.

The Earth does not miss seasons, they may take their time coming, but they get here. It's the same with us.

Have a blessed day!

September 17

The Earth wobbles because of the gravitational pull of outside forces pulling at the equatorial bulge. The Sun and the moon both pull at the Earth creating the wobble.

We wobble in faith and obedience to God for the same reason. The forces of darkness are pulling us in one direction, and the love of God is pulling us another.

So recognize why you are not perfect, but like the Earth, maintain your rotation around the Son and He will continue to rise in your life—despite the dark influences pulling at you.

God bless you.

September 18

*T*he weather in any particular season lags behind the start of the season because it takes the Earth some time to warm up or cool down.

So if God has told you this is a new season in your life, but you don't feel the effects— wait on the Lord. The hot situations will cool down, and things which cooled off will hear back up - in due season.

The Earth does not miss seasons, they may take their time coming, but they get here. It's the same with us.

Have a blessed day!

September 19

*T*he Earth wobbles because of the gravitational pull of outside forces pulling at the equatorial bulge. The Sun and the moon both pull at the Earth creating the wobble.

We wobble in faith and obedience to God for the same reason. The forces of darkness are pulling us in one direction, and the love of God is pulling us another.

So recognize why you are not perfect, but like the Earth, maintain your rotation around the Son and He will continue to rise in your life—despite the dark influences pulling at you.

God bless you.

HAPPY *Sunday!*

September 20

*F*lowers don't need umbrellas, they need rain. It helps them grow.

It's the same for us in certain situations we have to face. So don't be so quick to cover someone from a lesson they need to learn.

It may be needed to help them grow.

God bless you!

September 21

*K*nock-off religion is like knock-off clothes: obviously fake to the Maker and anyone wearing the real thing.

Check your spiritual labels and be sure they match Scripture!

Have a blessed day!

September 22

As children of God, we are all connected. So when you get out of something that was tough to go through, always look back and see if you can help someone else going through the same thing.

Connect with them.

That's brotherly love and it pleases God.

September 23

When it comes to wisdom, some aren't that fashionable—so model it for them today:

Colossians 4:5 - Walk in wisdom toward those who are without...

Show the whole world how God designed us to be.

Amen

September 24

W hen someone does you wrong and needs to be taught a lesson, make it a lesson about love and forgiveness:

1 Peter 3:9 NIV - Do not repay evil with evil or insult with insult. On the contrary, repay evil with blessing, because to this you were called so that you may inherit a blessing.

God bless you!

September 25

When a deer is in the dark and sees a bright light, it freezes and waits to see what the light will do. It doesn't know what to do with itself because it can no longer see its way, so it puts itself totally at the mercy of the light.

When the Light of God shines out of darkness upon us, we should do the same thing.

John 8:12 - Then spake Jesus again unto them, saying, I am the light of the world: he that followeth me shall not walk in darkness, but shall have the light of life.

HAPPY *Sunday!*

September 26

S ometimes, if not washed away, residual waste from things of which our bodies has rid itself, can cause itching behind us - if not properly washed away. It works the same way spiritually: if our sins are not properly washed away, we end up itching to do the things behind us, the sins from which we rid ourselves in our past.

Just wanted to show there is an answer in God's Word for everything:

1 Peter 3:15 - But sanctify the Lord God in your hearts: and be ready always to give an answer to every man that asketh you a reason of the hope that is in you with meekness and fear...

This may not help with the rear end but it will help in THE END.

September 27

*T*he Spirit that raised Jesus from the grave is the same Spirit that woke you up this morning and the same Spirit that will pull you out of any dead situation you wind up in:

Romans 8:11 - But if the Spirit of him that raised up Jesus from the dead dwell in you, he that raised up Christ from the dead shall also quicken your mortal bodies by his Spirit that dwelleth in you.

Amen

HAPPY *Sunday!*

September 28

*W*hen your "circle" starts going in circles, it might be time to take a break from your circle— even if you have to do it in a round-about way.

Proverbs 13:20 - He that walketh with wise men shall be wise: but a companion of fools shall be destroyed.

Let that circle in your spirit for a moment.

God bless you!

September 29

*T*he Spirit that raised Jesus from the grave is the same Spirit that woke you up this morning and the same Spirit that will pull you out of any dead situation you wind up in:

Romans 8:11 - But if the Spirit of him that raised up Jesus from the dead dwell in you, he that raised up Christ from the dead shall also quicken your mortal bodies by his Spirit that dwelleth in you.

Amen

HAPPY Sunday!

September 30

Mountains used to be measured from the ground up using levels and sighting devices to measure angles.

Now, they are measured more accurately from the sky down using satellite techniques.

Before coming to Christ, I used to measure the mountains I faced with varying levels of fear and doubt, looking for low angles to climb up and over.

I lived from the bottom up.

In Jesus, I've found a way to trust God and let Him determine the height and depth of my situations, looking to Him for help and strength to climb up and over everything I face.

I'm living from the top down.

October 1

*R*oots are the real beauty of a tree.

It's the same with people. So when seeking a beautiful person to love, look beneath the surface.

That's good advice from the Lord:

Song of Solomon 4:7 - Thou art all fair, my love; there is no spot in thee.

October 2

*F*reedom from bondage begins with loosing the things within you that are already free.

October 3

*U*nless you have two of them, your mouth should be used for one purpose: praise.

James 3:10 - Out of the same mouth proceedeth blessing and cursing. My brethren, these things ought not so to be.

Don't make God have to shut you up twice.

October 4

*Y*ou can't make people believe in God by making people believe in God. You can only make people believe you believe in God, which is what makes people believe in God, but what you believe can't be make believe— you have to really believe it.

So if you believe, then believe that.

October 5

*T*he doggie paddle is an effective way to stay afloat and not drown so it's okay to imitate it, but it's not necessary to imitate other dog characteristics to do it.

It's the same in our Christian walk. There are some effective worldly principles we can accept and use in order to stay afloat and not drown. That is because they are based upon Godly principles; the others we can throw out and leave in the world.

Remember to separate the meat from the bones and the seeds from the fruit. Be in the world, but not of the world.

Amen

HAPPY *Sunday!*

October 6

*I*n football, runners point out defensive players they want their teammates to block and move out of their way. It's the most effective way to evade those trying to tackle you and bring you down.

In life, Believers run for Jesus and the prize of the high calling found in Him. When people or things try to stop us and bring us down, we, too, should point them out to God and He will block them or move them out of our way.

So have faith, keep running, for Jesus, and pray about (point out) any obstacles in the way.

God Bless You!

October 7

*F*orks in the road are shaped like a Y.

Why?

Because you should always know Y you are going in the direction you choose.

Proverbs 4:26 - Ponder the path of thy feet, and let all thy ways be established.

Make wise decisions and take wise paths.

God bless you.

October 8

*T*ortoises hide inside their hard shells.

People who are slow to respond to love and affection are similar—they hide in their hard shells.

Accept the love and kindness God is showing you through others.

Today, come out, come out, wherever you are.

God bless you!

October 9

*A*s the nation of Israel traveled to Promised Land God prescribed they rest and build monuments to memorialize certain occasions, forever engraving them into memory.

That was for their good. It was a good thing.

As you walk with God, you should be sure to rest and create monumental memories that you will always remember.

HAPPY *Sunday!*

October 10

N ewton's First Law of Motion states that in order for the motion of an object to change, a force must act upon it, a concept generally called inertia.

The first law if the Spirit shows us that in order for the life of a person to change for the better, the Spirit must move upon it, a concept generally called sanctification.

October 11

N ewton's Third Law of Motion states that any time a force acts from one object to another, there is an equal force acting back on the original object. If you pull on a rope, therefore, the rope is pulling back on you as well.

So don't try to pull people into Church because they'll only pull back. Just give your testimony of how good The Lord is, and allow God to use an unequal force (one much greater) to do the pulling in.

October 12

Potential energy is energy stored up for action—as in a stretched rubber band or squeezed spring.

So if you're in a tight squeeze or things are stretched thin, remember, in God, you always have the potential to snap back in order and spring into good shape.

October 13

Shocked that one of your idols has fallen?

Don't be:

Micah 5:13 NIV - I will destroy your idols and your sacred stones from among you; you will no longer bow down to the work of your hands.

Whatever you stand up next to God is going to get pulled down when it gets too tall.

HAPPY *Sunday!*

October 14

C hristians are like streetlight posts. We are not the Light but we hold Him up to illuminate those who cross our paths.

October 15

T he curb is higher than the streets to signal where the street ends and to help see the boundaries for the way one is traveling.

Likewise, when we come to Christ we curb some of the street behaviors we have and set new boundaries that transition us from the fast life and align us with our walk with God.

October 16

*I*mitation is the best form of flattery.

Flatter Jesus today.

October 17

*W*ater begins to boil at 212 degrees at sea level. However, the higher up you go, the higher the temperature must be for water to boil.

It's the same for our boiling points. As we elevate our minds and hearts in Christ, it takes longer for things to anger and agitate us.

So elevate, and have a blessed day!

October 18

*O*ur sight is designed in a manner that makes roads and paths seem to taper off and end in the distance. We see what appears to be the end of the road in every path we view.

Knowing this, always walk by faith, or you won't be inclined to go anywhere because it will always seem like there is nowhere to go.

I love you. Have a blessed day!

October 19

*T*here are times we can be pointed in the right direction but still be going the wrong way.

That is why sometimes it appears that the more progress we make the further we seem to move away from our destination.

Ask God to order your steps.

October 20

*L*ike childhood teddy bears, grudges look silly when you hold onto them too long.

1 Corinthians 13:11 – ...when I became a man, I put away childish things.

Whatever childish thing you're still carrying, be mature about it and let it go.

October 21

*A*s with icicles hanging from a tree, God can stop things from falling even in the middle of the fall.

That includes you:

Jude 1:24 - Now unto him that is able to keep you from falling, and to present you faultless before the presence of his glory with exceeding joy,

Amen

HAPPY *Sunday!*

October 22

*I*n a world full of peaks and valleys its best to always take the high road.

It may twist and turn, but it will get you to where you're going in an elevated manner.

October 23

*T*he chicken came before the egg. That is why the chicken sits on the egg.

Likewise, be on top of things as a parent and raise your children, instead of them raising you.

You are in charge—so don't be too chicken act like it.

October 24

*T*he world may say you're condemned, but God will never let them demolish you.

In His eyes you're under reconstruction.

October 25

a triangle has three sides. The sum of the angles within a triangle always equal 180 degrees, regardless of the size or shape of the triangle.

180 degrees is a complete turn.

To sum things up—spiritually speaking—The Father, Son, and Holy Spirit can create an about face in your life regardless of the size or shape of your problem.

No matter what angle you look at it, that too, is a complete turn.

Have a blessed day!

October 26

*N*o matter how big it is or how you slice it, if Jesus is your portion—you have the biggest peace.

John 14:27 - Peace I leave with you, my peace I give unto you: not as the world giveth, give I unto you. Let not your heart be troubled, neither let it be afraid.

October 27

*Y*es, there is a lot on your plate followed by a few things that are tough to swallow, but God never gives us more than we can chew.

Trust Him and take one bite a time. Somehow He'll make things easier to digest.

Have a blessed day.

Amen

October 28

R oot to fruit...

If we root ourselves in the values of the those who raised us, those same values will blossom in those we raise.

October 29

T he waves behind you determine how you got here. The waves in front of you determine where you're going.

So if you're not yet where you plan to be, keep making waves.

October 30

*W*hen is it too soon to give up believing what God said would happen?

Always.

Amen

October 31

*S*ome don't focus on doing their best work because they don't believe it pays, but when God sees one working hard for others, one sees God working hard for them.

So do all you as if you're doing it for God:

Ephesians 6:8 - Knowing that whatsoever any man doeth, the same shall receive of the Lord...

And remember, the supervisor may pass out the work, but it's the Boss who signs the checks.

November 1

*W*e are the temple of God. He dwells within us. We house His praise, worship, and purposes. But when you abandon God, He abandons you; and remember, abandoned houses are demolished.
Stay filled with His presence.
God Bless You!

November 2

*C*onfession is like soap. It brings up our dirt so God's forgiveness can wash it away and make us clean:

John 1:9 - If we confess our sins, he is faithful and just to forgive us *our* sins, and to cleanse us from all unrighteousness.

How else can God forgive you, if you don't bring up what you've done wrong?

God Bless You!

November 3

*T*wo times has Jesus stood at a tomb door—

from the inside (His tomb) and the outside (Lazarus' tomb)—and on both occasions someone walked out of the of the grave.

Are you in a dead situation with seemingly no way out?

Look to Jesus— you'll be walking out of it in not time.

November 4

*T*he devil's deconstruction permit only applies to material things. Build your hopes on things eternal.

Construct a life of treasures (faith, hope, love) that thieves cannot steal, moths do not devour, and rust will not wear away.

And don't forget to put your heart into it:

Matthew 6:21 - For where your treasure is, there will your heart be also.

Amen

November 5

*I*f Jesus has performed a miracle in your life before, you can count on him to perform another one. It's biblical:

John 4:54 - This is again the second miracle *that* Jesus did...

So have faith and keep counting on him.

November 6

*P*eople often attempt to find themselves under Mistletoe because of the great things that are supposed to happen when you stand under it.

However, despite the romanticism surrounding it, Mistletoe is a poisonous parasite and can be deadly if it or its berries are ingested.

It's the same with sin. The stories we're told about it are enticing, however it will poison and suck the life out of you in the same fashion as Mistletoe.

Don't stand under either one. If you want love, stand under Jesus Christ.

November 7

*T*wo times has Jesus stood at a tomb door—from the inside (His tomb) and the outside (Lazarus' tomb)—and on both occasions someone walked out of the of the grave.

Are you in a dead situation with seemingly no way out?

Look to Jesus— you'll be walking out of it in not time.

November 8

*T*he word erosion comes from the Latin word 'erosionem' which means 'a gnawing away.'

Sin erodes the foundation of faith. It gnaws away at it until there is nothing left. So turn from sin immediately, before it erodes your fellowship with God and leaves you with

November 9

*I*s it just me or sometimes does it seem like it's a secret between you and God just how much He loves you and how important you are?

Anyway, I hope it's not really a secret because I just can't keep it to myself!

God loves us so much. Remember that and have a blessed day!

November 10

*I*f you look to the hills and see problems racing toward you, have faith and be still. You'll soon see that they are racing at you but God is chasing them past you:

Psalm 121:21-22 - I will lift up mine eyes unto the hills, from whence cometh my help. My help cometh from the LORD, which made heaven and earth.

So whatever appears to be coming at you today, keep trusting and looking to God until it passes by you.

HAPPY *Sunday!*

November 11

*T*here are those who only reach out when they are sure you can't reach back.

Beware of false-giving and the false-givers.

Really help.

Seek real help.

November 12

*I*f you are looking for thanks don't look to people because you may or may not get it. Do what you do in the name of God and look to Him instead:

Hebrews 6:10 - For God is not unrighteous to forget your work and labour of love, which ye have shewed toward his name...

November 13

W hen you tell someone you're "going to be the bigger person," it actually makes you the smaller person.

There is no ascension in condescension. If you're trying to make peace, be sincere and make it peacefully.

November 14

*T*urtle shells seem to make turtles invincible but actually they have nerves and veins embedded in them, which means they can bleed and even cause the turtle to feel pain in them.

It is the same with people. Some people seem hard and invincible because of their character and disposition, however, like everyone else they have feelings, too. Saying or doing mean and hurtful things to them causes as much pain in them as anybody else.

So don't base how you treat people on how they appear on the outside, because we're all the same inside.

Just be nice to everybody—that way no one gets hurt.

Because Every Day is "Son" day.

November 15

*T*he first chance you get, take a chance and give a chance to the second chance you have in Jesus.

If by chance this is the first chance you've really taken a chance to consider it, don't take a chance and not take this chance because even though there is a second chance, no one knows the last chance, and there may not be another chance to take this chance again.

You've had your chance and tried all you can do; now give Jesus a chance and take His second chance while you still have a chance.

It takes a second, but if you give it a chance, what you just read will bless you (and not just by chance).

SCAN ME

November 16

*C*aterpillars have so many legs because it takes a lot of steps to become a butterfly.

Remember that when you get weary on the road to your goals.

November 17

*D*on't bury the hatchet with the handle sticking out. When you forgive someone, really forgive them.

November 18

*G*od does not have a loss column—because there is only victory in Jesus.

November 19

*T*he comfort of walking a difficult path is in the road you create for those behind you.

Proverbs 17:7 NIV - Whoever heeds discipline shows the way to life, but whoever ignores correction leads others astray.

November 20

*N*othing is certain. You just have to trust God and keep walking the path He provides.

Ecclesiastes 7:14 NLT - Enjoy prosperity while you can, but when hard times strike, realize that both come from God. Remember that nothing is certain in this life.

HAPPY *Sunday!*

November 21

*T*he devil is coming at you with new weapons every day. Why are you using your old lifestyle to fight him?

Upgrade to new life in Christ, and start using spiritual weapons. Then you'll stop losing the battle.

II Corinthians 10:4 NIV - The weapons we fight with are not the weapons of the world. On the contrary, they have divine power to demolish strongholds.

God bless you!

November 22

*W*hen you fill yourself with the actions of certain words they tend to belong to you. For example:

Joy belongs to the joyful, peace belongs to the peaceful, and faith belongs to the faithful.

Likewise hate belongs to the hateful, spite belongs to the spiteful, and pity belongs to the pitiful.

You are where you are because you're full of something, and as long as you're full of it - you will be where you belong.

I hope you have a blessed day, and that is why I am hopeful.

November 23

*W*hen you see teeth, don't always take it as someone is smiling at you— it can also mean you're about to get bit.

Just be careful in your dealings. Everyone is not your friend.

Matthew 10:16 Behold, I send you forth as sheep in the midst of wolves: be ye therefore wise as serpents, and harmless as doves.

November 24

*L*earn how to exercise your faith:

When you let yourself down, bend your knees (in prayer) and pull yourself up (in faith).

You'll rise from point A (feeling down) to point B (feeling up), getting stronger with every repetition.

November 25

*J*ust like a cheap rug, wealth as can be pulled from under you.

Stand on the word of God, not how much money you have.

Proverbs 23:5 - Wilt thou set thine eyes upon that which is not? for riches certainly make themselves wings...

HAPPY *Sunday!*

November 26

*W*alking stick bugs are insects that mimic the appearance of the branches on which they live. When the seasons change and the foliage color changes, the walking stick will change its diet so as to continue matching its environment. Unless it moves or casts a shadow, its predators don't know it's even there.

Believers that stick with their walk with God are the same way. Seasons may change, but we adjust to God's will, and continue to follow His Word. Unless we move in our own understanding, or cast shadows of doubt at His promises—the Devourer is always thwarted.

Mimic the walking stick.

Stick with God. Walk with Him.

November 27

*I*n Christ, we are all one and part of the Body. Everybody is somebody.

So, don't treat anybody like nobody.

I Corinthians 12:14 - For the body is not one member, but many.

God bless you!

HAPPY *Sunday!*

November 28

D resser crabs have an interesting way of surviving. They accessorize themselves with their environment. As they move through the water they scan the ground for objects that match their environment and attach them to their Velcro-like skins.

Sure, it's a great disguise and defense mechanism but you never see what they really look like.

Some people are like dresser crabs. They do whatever it takes to match the situations and people that surround them without ever being themselves.

Sure, sometimes it helps them get ahead in life, but you never know who they really are.

Don't be a dresser crab. Be who God made you to be. Trust that He'll keep you and help you succeed in whatever environment He leads you.

November 29

*H*ow do you love an elephant? The same way we should love one another, one hug at a time.

Smile and have a blessed day, full of these types of hugs.

November 30

*Y*ou don't have to worry about saving face for sins you've done in the past. Jesus died for all of them, and has given you a new face.

Face it, God has forgiven you.

HAPPY *Sunday!*

December 1

I like thighs that rub together. Wait, let me explain:

They remind me of good friends. No matter what life pulls on them stick to each other and press through, until their back together and in touch again.

Nothing that comes between them lasts forever. They always find a way to wear it down and keep in touch—even when things are layered on.

Thank God for making fat thighs and reminding us to stick together.

I love my friends and the way the rub off on me.

God bless you, your good friends, and your fat thighs.

December 2

A smile is not straight. It's curved, and therefore crooked.

So if you must do something crooked today, make it a smile.

Think about that for a minute. It will help straighten you out.

December 3

*I*f a preacher never steps on your toes, he isn't dancing to the beat of God's drum.

Avoid teachers that dance around sin so that you don't end up out of step with God's Word.

December 4

*W*ant to learn how to speak in the Spirit?

Say, "Jesus is Lord."

There you go.

1 Corinthians 12:3 - ...no man can say Jesus is Lord, but by the Holy Ghost.

December 5

*O*ut of all the birds that fly in the sky only owls can see it as blue.

Out of all the people that have been told about God only Believers see it as true.

Owls and Believers are peculiar and wise.

December 6

a leech has 32 brains. In fact, all freeload-ers have enough sense to take care of them-selves, so don't let them bleed you dry.

2 Thessalonians 3:10 - ...if any would not work, neither should he eat.

December 7

*T*he typical pencil can draw a line 35 miles long.

So it's never too late to draw the line and stop doing something you shouldn't be do-ing—even if you've been doing it a long time, just draw a long line.

December 8

*T*hank you God for giving me things I didn't even know to ask for, and for doing things for me I never even imagined you would do:

Jude 1:24 - Now unto him that is able to do exceeding abundantly above all that we ask or think, according to the power that worketh in us, Unto him be glory in the church by Christ Jesus throughout all ages, world without end.

December 9

*T*his is Y O U before praying.

This is YOU after praying.

Praying gets YOU together.

Pray.

December 10

*H*olding on is the same as being knotted together. So if you've tied the knot, keep holding on.

Mark 10:9 - What therefore God hath joined together, let not man put asunder.

December 11

*M*ost tornados are visible, but there are some that can't be seen.

Remember that when storms rise up and suddenly things are twisted, and you don't see nor understand why and how.

Treat these times like tornadoes—take cover under the shelter of God and wait for them to pass.

December 12

*W*e all have a bridge to cross to get to the other side, and we all have to choose sides as we cross it.

The side chosen by us on this side of the bridge reflects the side chosen for us on the other side of the bridge.

Remember that.

Amen.

December 13

N o matter what you face, always remember who is behind you and what He has already done:

Deuteronomy 1:20 - When thou goest out to battle against thine enemies, and seest horses, and chariots, and a people more than thou, be not afraid of them: for the LORD thy God is with thee, which brought thee up out of the land of Egypt.

Have a confident and victorious day.

Amen

HAPPY *Sunday!*

December 14

a ir passing through the naval cavity (your nose) is warmed or cooled to match your body temperature inside.

Likewise, busybodies and nosy people change the information they hear and gather to match what they are already thinking inside.

This is good to know and explains a lot of things.

December 15

*B*ears hibernate in the winter, and when resting they do not defecate.

Believers rest in the Lord and when resting they don't start mess, either (or at least they shouldn't).

Bear with me and pardon the bathroom pun, but get my point?

If you're supposed to be resting in the Lord, don't start any mess today.

December 16

$a$ir passing through the naval cavity (your nose) is warmed or cooled to match your body temperature inside.

Likewise, busybodies and nosy people change the information they hear and gather to match what they are already thinking inside.

This is good to know and explains a lot of things.

December 17

*W*hat God gives is to be given: we are loved so we can love, healed so we can heal, forgiven so we can forgive, blessed so we can bless, comforted so we can comfort, and so on.

It is God's works that flow to us and through us, and not our own:

2 Corinthians 1:3,4 - Blessed be God, even the Father of our Lord Jesus Christ, the Father of mercies, and the God of all comfort; Who comforteth us in all our tribulation, that we may be able to comfort them which are in any trouble, by the comfort wherewith we ourselves are comforted of God.

So thank God for the comforts you have received by passing them along to others.

December 18

*T*he hair and blubber on a polar bear is ten inches thick. That's why they act so oblivious to the frigidity of their environment.

We, too, should learn to have thicker skin when dealing with cold-hearted people.

December 19

*T*he average person has about 70,000 thoughts a day. So if you say you love God, but haven't thought about thanking or praising Him all day, please do the math and recognize you're not fooling Him, only yourself. Give God the honor, glory, and praise due His Holy Name today—while you're thinking about it.

December 20

$\mathcal{I}$f you can look back and see that not everybody could have or did make it over the obstacles you've faced, that alone is enough to give God praise.

December 21

$\mathcal{I}$t costs more than a penny to make a penny.

With that in mind, consider the value of what you value because not everything is worth its value. There really are some things that are not worth doing.

So before you do things, ask yourself: Is it

HAPPY *Sunday!*

December 22

Spiritually speaking, there are no empty dirty laundry baskets in this world. We all have something that needs washing.

Keep that in your spin cycle and have a blessed day!

December 23

For every human killed by a shark, two million sharks are killed by humans. Yet condemnation is placed upon sharks.

With that in mind answer this question:

For every evil act committed against you, how many evil things are you doing as you condemn others?

That is something to ponder.

December 24

D opamine and serotonin are released in the pleasure center of your brain when you take drugs to get high.

Dopamine and serotonin are also released in the pleasure center of your brain when you give to those in need and when you help others.

The lesson to learn? You don't have to get high in life to get high on life.

Do good and help others today. Get as high on life as you can.

December 25

U nless you have a degenerative brain disease like Alzheimer's or dementia, your brain never loses the ability to learn and change.

So if you're thinking what you're thinking is what you'll always be thinking because you can't change your thinking—think again.

Now think about what you should change and change your thinking.

December 26

Y our peripheral vision improves at night. Perhaps that is why the side effects of sin become so visible after the dark impacts of sin kick-in.

That's just a dark thought (that gives light) to consider.

December 27

B efore you put on that makeup please note:

A research study conducted by Orbit Complete discovered that 69% of people find women more attractive when they smile than when they are wearing makeup.

So whatever you plan to apply to that beautiful face of yours, remember to smile and have a blessed day!

December 28

B efore you start worrying about everything please read and meditate upon this:

Philippians 4:6 New Living Translation – "Don't worry about anything; instead, pray about everything. Tell God what you need, and thank him for all he has done."

Now have a blessed day.

December 29

$\mathcal{B}$ utterflies cannot fly if their body temperature is less than 86°.

In the same vein, it's hard for cold hearted people to elevate themselves in the eyes of others.

So if you want other people to stop looking down on you, you'll have to be a little bit warmer.

December 30

$\mathcal{B}$ lue whales are the largest creatures to have ever lived on the earth, yet they eat (and get filled by) the smallest creatures in the sea, tiny shrimp-like creatures called krill.

So as you chase down big things for self-satisfaction, remember: the biggest hearts are filled with joy by the smallest things.

December 31

W aking up is proof that God has not abandoned you.

The possibilities are endless from here—seek them.

Stacey Sartin

Stacey Sartin is a fifth-generation preacher of the Good News of Jesus Christ. He and wife Kaneisha are Pastor and First Lady of New Jerusalem Missionary Baptist Church in Detroit, Michigan, USA. *Happy Sunday* is the second book in the Arrows of Deliverance series, a fascinating read of spiritual truths through the lenses of science, nature, and common sense. The first book, Arrows of Deliverance, was published in 2014. Since it's publication, Pastor Stacey has taught, mentored, and preached these truths through the community, in addition to posting over 10,000 inspirational messages of hope, faith, and perseverance on social media. All of this, including the publication of the book you're now holding, is spited by the hope that all will clearly see that in Christ Jesus every day is "SON" Day!

CPSIA information can be obtained
at www.ICGtesting.com
Printed in the USA
FSHW022213081120

9 780578 782874